Ward A. Knights Jr., MDiv, STM, DD

Pastoral Counseling
A Gestalt Approach

Pre-publication
REVIEWS,
COMMENTARIES,
EVALUATIONS . . .

"I find Ward Knights' book on integrating the concepts of Gestalt therapy with pastoral counseling most fascinating. It opens new vistas for counseling not emphasized in other therapeutic practices, such as the staying in the here and now; learning to communicate directly in the I-Thou mind-set; avoiding 'aboutism'—talking about a situation instead of reliving the scenario and relating to the people in one's life; and becoming aware of the many different parts of ourselves and integrating mind, body, heart, and spirit. Ward Knights has given pastoral counselors a remarkable tool for helping people grow, not only psychosocially, but also spiritually."

Rabbi Harold (Chaim) Richter
Director of Chaplaincy (Retired),
Jewish Federation of Broward,
Florida

"Dr. Knights has put together a concise overview of Gestalt theory and practice, integrating it into the pastoral care and counseling that many clergy use in their day-to-day ministry. He has done an admirable service by providing a rich resource for students in seminaries and clinical pastoral education programs. For students or clergy who are contemplating application to a clinical pastoral education program, this work is an excellent introduction to the theory and practice of pastoral care on a more profound level. Knights' writing style is personal and illustrative, weaving theological and scriptural concepts with Fritz Perls' Gestalt therapy, which is confrontative, yet supportive intervention. This is a needed emphasis for clergy to hear in their counseling, namely, get at the issue now and work it through now, so one may be released for better living and greater ministry."

Reverend Raymond A. Otto, DMin
Director of Pastoral Care
and Supervisor of Clinical
Pastoral Education,
Jackson Health System,
Miami, Florida

More pre-publication
REVIEWS, COMMENTARIES, EVALUATIONS . . .

"In its application of Gestalt principles to the spiritual striving for inner wholeness, this book is a benefit to any reader interested in the link between psychology and religion. Encouragement is also offered to pastoral representatives for the development of a vitality in their lives so that their pastoral presence becomes a here and now resource to parishioners. Even though some pastors may not choose to utilize some of the specific Gestalt approaches in their pastoral role, the principles underlying this form of therapy provide helpful insights about the human hopes for spiritual aliveness. The material further serves as a resourceful primer in depicting very capably the history of Gestalt therapy and its founder, Fritz Perls.

This informative publication offers rich insights not only for parish pastors and specialized pastoral psychotherapists, but also for academic use in pastoral care and counseling courses. Also, disciplines from the other helping professions, such as psychology, can gain from the illumination that Knights sheds on this vital bridge between the Gestalt tradition and the religious life."

Thomas A. Summers, DMin
Clinical Pastoral Education Supervisor, Columbia, South Carolina

"In a time when life for many people is lived in a sense of being 'broken off,' the pastoral counselor is faced with the urgent need of guiding parishioners to closure of life events and wholeness of life itself. Ward A. Knights has provided an introduction to Gestalt in *Pastoral Counseling: A Gestalt Approach*. The key element of present-tense awareness is highlighted. Techniques and experiments in Gestalt methodologies and dream work produce a practical introduction to the actual practice of the method. Verbatims of sessions include 'hot spot' moments when parishioners and CPE students were urged to encounter and even talk to themselves and experience elements of their dreams. There is even a sermon.

This book will be useful as an ancillary text in more advanced pastoral counseling and care courses, a must for the theological library, and a meaningful addition to the shelves of the practicing clergy. Where else could we see people be a train, yell at God, pound pillows, and in the end emerge with a new awareness of themselves through the Gestalt approach?"

David Gasperson, PhD
Academic Dean,
South Florida Center
for Theological Studies, Miami

The Haworth Pastoral Press®
An Imprint of The Haworth Press, Inc.
New York • London • Oxford

NOTES FOR PROFESSIONAL LIBRARIANS AND LIBRARY USERS

This is an original book title published by The Haworth Pastoral Press®, an imprint of The Haworth Press, Inc. Unless otherwise noted in specific chapters with attribution, materials in this book have not been previously published elsewhere in any format or language.

CONSERVATION AND PRESERVATION NOTES

All books published by The Haworth Press, Inc. and its imprints are printed on certified pH neutral, acid free book grade paper. This paper meets the minimum requirements of American National Standard for Information Sciences-Permanence of Paper for Printed Material, ANSI Z39.48-1984.

Pastoral Counseling
A Gestalt Approach

THE HAWORTH PASTORAL PRESS

Religion and Mental Health
Harold G. Koenig, MD
Senior Editor

New, Recent, and Forthcoming Titles:

Adventures in Senior Living: Learning How to Make Retirement Meaningful and Enjoyable by J. Lawrence Driskill

Dying, Grieving, Faith, and Family: A Pastoral Care Approach by George W. Bowman

The Pastoral Care of Depression: A Guidebook by Binford W. Gilbert

Understanding Clergy Misconduct in Religious Systems: Scapegoating, Family Secrets, and the Abuse of Power by Candace R. Benyei

What the Dying Teach Us: Lessons on Living by Samuel Lee Oliver

The Pastor's Family: The Challenges of Family Life and Pastoral Responsibilities by Daniel L. Langford

Somebody's Knocking at Your Door: AIDS and the African-American Church by Ronald Jeffrey Weatherford and Carole Boston Weatherford

Grief Education for Caregivers of the Elderly by Junietta Baker McCall

The Obsessive-Compulsive Disorder: Pastoral Care for the Road to Change by Robert M. Collie

The Pastoral Care of Children by David H. Grossoehme

Ways of the Desert: Becoming Holy Through Difficult Times by William F. Kraft

Caring for a Loved One with Alzheimer's Disease: A Christian Perspective by Elizabeth T. Hall

"Martha, Martha": How Christians Worry by Elaine Leong Eng

Spiritual Care for Children Living in Specialized Settings: Breathing Underwater by Michael F. Friesen

Broken Bodies, Healing Hearts: Reflections of a Hospital Chaplain by Gretchen W. TenBrook

Shared Grace: Therapists and Clergy Working Together by Marion Bilich, Susan Bonfiglio, and Steven Carlson

The Pastor's Guide to Psychiatric Disorders and Mental Health Resources by W. Brad Johnson and William L. Johnson

Christ-Centered Therapy: Empowering the Self by Russ Harris

Bioethics from a Faith Perspective: Ethics in Health Care for the Twenty-First Century by Jack Hanford

Pastoral Counseling: A Gestalt Approach by Ward A. Knights

Family Abuse and the Bible. The Scriptural Perspective by Aimee K. Cassiday-Shaw

When the Caregiver Becomes the Patient: A Journey from a Mental Disorder to Recovery and Compassionate Insight by Daniel L. Langford and Emil J. Authelet

A Theology of God Talk: The Language of the Heart by J. Timothy Allen

A Practical Guide to Hospital Ministry: Healing Ways by Junietta B. McCall

Pastoral Counseling
A Gestalt Approach

Ward A. Knights Jr., MDiv, STM, DD

The Haworth Pastoral Press®
An Imprint of The Haworth Press, Inc.
New York • London • Oxford

Published by

The Haworth Pastoral Press®, an imprint of The Haworth Press, Inc., 10 Alice Street, Binghamton, NY 13904-1580.

Cover design by Anastasia Litwak.

Library of Congress Cataloging-in-Publication Data

Knights, Ward A., 1927-
Pastoral counseling : a Gestalt approach / Ward A. Knights, Jr.
p. cm.
Includes bibliographical references and index.
ISBN 0-7890-1531-5 (alk. paper)—ISBN 0-7890-1532-3 (alk. paper)
1. Pastoral counseling. 2. Gestalt therapy. I. Title.

BV4012.2 .K59 2002
253.5—dc21

2001039107

CONTENTS

Foreword **ix**

Robert H. Olin, MD

Preface **xi**

Chapter 1. A Meeting at the Center of Vital Awareness **1**

The Gestalt Perspective 3
Attention = Awareness = Expressiveness = Closure 4
Gestalt and Christian Perspectives 6
Pastoral Care—An Illustration 10

Chapter 2. Becoming Fully Human **13**

How We Block Our Experience 15
Here and Now 24

Chapter 3. Peeling the Onion **29**

Rules 31
Games 35
Other Resources 39
A Perspective on Psychodynamics 42

Chapter 4. Once Upon a Time **49**

Gestalting the Folktale 51
Meanwhile, Back at the Castle 54

Chapter 5. A Taste of Our Own Medicine **57**

Awareness 57
Gestalt Experiments 58
The Hot Seat 62
Beyond the Hot Seat 68

Chapter 6. The Royal Road to Integration **71**

Dream Work 71
Catching the Train 74
Crystal Chandeliers 80

Chapter 7. Where the Rubber Hits the Road **85**

Background 85
The Counseling Session 88
Analysis 94

Chapter 8. We Are Fallible Human Beings **103**

Appendix. A Biographical Sketch of Frederick S. Perls, MD, PhD (1894-1970) **109**

Notes **115**

Index **119**

ABOUT THE AUTHOR

Ward A. Knights Jr., MDiv, STM, DD, is a Unitarian Universalist minister and a qualified Gestalt therapist. He earned his doctorate in pastoral theology and counseling from Vanderbilt University. He earned his MDiv and STM at Andover-Newton Theological School and his BA from John Brown University. He did his Gestalt training at The Gestalt Institute of Cleveland, The Gestalt Institute of Houston, and The Gestalt Institute of Minnesota.

Dr. Knights is the author of numerous articles and books. He has served as parish minister, hospital chaplain, military chaplain, Gestalt psychotherapist, supervisor of clinical pastoral education, and member of the faculty at a theological school.

Foreword

It once came to me in a moment of truth to "Never say anything bad about anyone." Yet, I asked myself, if I never say anything bad about anyone, how can I define all those awful things people do and tell them about it so they will stop? How will I make conversation with other people if I don't discuss bad behaviors?

The attempt to implement this rule has changed my entire approach to psychotherapy. I have given up my traditional view that one must get patients to acknowledge and give up their defenses, resolve or break down their armor, and notice their counterproductive behavior. Instead, I have discovered all I need to do is help people define who they are—in depth. Consequently, all the defenses, armor, and counterproductive behavior fall away by themselves. I believe this occurs because when we focus on defenses we are not seeing the true picture, but an obscured strand of identity—perhaps like looking at a twig on end. The key to defining identity is to be able to see through the defense or armor. These defenses give us a limited understanding of the client's attempt to define his or her authentic self. When we get a three-dimensional view of the defenses, it isn't a defense at all but an end-view of a strand of identity. This strand of identity presents itself in this manner because it is unclear to the client and is trying to surface in his consciousness—coming up end-first rather than broadside. The change of my therapeutic approach was a result of a spiritual insight rather than a scientific insight.

It was only in afterthought that I saw how similar defining "who people are," rather than "who they are not," (their defenses) is similar to Jesus' belief in seeing the good in people. He believed in turning one's back on evil, rather than engaging it in an encounter or fight.

We all seek to define ourselves. It is only when we are afraid of what we might find that we become defensive. No loss is greater than the loss of who we are. Thus, recovering this loss allows us to face anything. Although the anguish of facing oneself can be tremendous, it makes all of life's problems—even injury and death—eventually an experience of peaceful awareness. Jesus knew this and it gave him the strength to walk straight to death.

Ward Knights has inserted Gestalt into a spiritual approach to counseling. It is a therapy which gets down to the very roots of our being—into the fluid, undifferentiated self where past/present/future and inner/outer meet as one, and yet differentiate.

It is gratifying to see Knights take the bull by the horns and grapple with the Gestalt approach from a spiritual position. I think he has produced a fine body of information, not only as it relates to spiritual and pastoral counseling, but also as an excellent primer in Gestalt. Fritz Perls, in his break from psychoanalysis, focused on how our current life choices fulfill our needs rather than looking for a past memory to account for personal problems. Knights does an excellent job of presenting this approach, as well as some new post–Fritz Perls concepts, in an unusually clear, easy-to-understand manner.

Robert H. Olin, MD
Director, Gestalt Therapy Institute of Minnesota

Preface

This book is about pastoral care and counseling from a particular perspective known as the Gestalt approach. What I have attempted to do is to share some of my own thinking and experience in bringing Gestalt, pastoral care, and counseling together. This is a process that I have been involved in for over three decades as a pastor, pastoral counselor, clinical pastoral educator, and Gestaltist.

We are currently witnessing a resurgence of activity and interest in Gestalt. The first Gestalt Institute was founded in New York City in 1952 and another in Cleveland in 1954. The increase in training centers has been phenomenal. The current Gestalt Directory now lists thirty-one Gestalt training centers in the United States alone with an additional twenty in other countries. These training centers offer a wide variety of programs from one-day workshops to three-year programs leading to certification as a Gestalt psychotherapist. Gestalt therapists are found in forty states as well as twenty-two foreign countries. In 1999, the International Gestalt Therapy Association was formed. It is an organization dedicated to the promotion and enrichment of Gestalt therapy on a worldwide basis. The IGTA has announced its Inaugural Conference to be held in August 2002 in Montreal, Quebec, Canada. *The Gestalt Therapy Journal* has been in continuous publication for two decades, and Gestalt is very active on the World Wide Web. It is a very exciting time, indeed!

In sharing what I do here, I have purposely chosen to put experience first and theory second, insofar as that is possible in a book. As we shall see from the Gestalt perspective, our experience is far more important than mere statements made about that experience. Yet, I hope that there is enough theoretical undergirding so that this book will help the reader enter more fully into personal experience, especially religious experience. I have made no effort to be profound, following the lead of Fritz Perls who believed that any understanding of human behavior should be capable of being put in simple terms.

In the examples that I have used, I have taken every precaution that no confidence be violated. Also, no material is shared that would make it possible to identify any individual.

My own understanding, experience, and training in relation to Gestalt have come from three sources: the Gestalt Institute of Cleveland, where I was first introduced to the Gestalt approach, and where I grew considerably through my involvement in the postgraduate program for psychotherapists, especially through my contact with Erving and Miriam Polster and Joseph Zinker; the Gestalt Institute of Houston, where it was my good fortune to work with Mary Ann Merksema, Ken Brennon, and Leland Johnson; and the Gestalt Therapy Institute of Minnesota where I was in therapy and training for several years.

I want to give a special word of appreciation to Robert H. Olin, MD, Director of the Gestalt Therapy Institute of Minnesota at the time of my affiliation there, who took the time to read this manuscript, and who helped me in several ways, especially in writing the section dealing with confluence.

Chapter 1

A Meeting at the Center of Vital Awareness

As a pastor, when I am with people my intention is that our meeting will be at the center of their vital awareness, a meeting which accurately and meaningfully contacts them literally where they are at that moment. Paul E. Johnson, one of the pioneers in modern pastoral care and counseling, referred to this stance as empathic and emphasized the necessity of the pastor beginning at this point if deepening levels of communication were to occur.[1]

I believe that the pastor's work involves meeting people at the center of vital awareness to explore spiritual growth with them. While I will have more to say about this later, I think that it is important to state this very clearly at the beginning. Charles Kemp has aptly referred to this basic identification of the pastor as being a "physician of the soul."[2] It is in relation to this task that the pastor seeks a better understanding of people and more effective ways of helping them.

Contemporary psychology and psychotherapy offer new understandings and tools for the pastor. But as the pastor looks around, there is a bewildering array of possible models of understanding and working with people. Orlo Strunk has surveyed these various approaches, both traditional and avant-garde, and notes their variety and complexity.[3] Which one ought the pastor to follow?

Psychoanalytic (Freudian) counselors suggest that if we can find the original cause of a problem, all will be well; client-centered counselors imply that only if we listen well to a person can that person find himself or herself; the rational-emotive approach seems to says that if we straighten out our thinking, all else will follow; primal therapy promotes abandonment of emotional control as the path to authenticity; encounter groups promise that great things will happen to us if we join a group and "let it all hang out"; and chemotherapy seems to imply that it is all chemical balances in the final analysis. The list goes on and on. It is patently obvious that no one of these approaches can be entirely right, can be *the* approach to use. Are they all wrong? I think not. Speaking from my own personal experience, I can say that each of these approaches makes a contribution to the achievement of human wholeness. At one time or another, I have participated in many of these approaches. Some I have experienced only as a dilettante, others I have studied extensively. I have found much that has helped me as a person and pastor. It is as though each has added another piece to the puzzle of human experience, human growth.

For example, I can remember how important it was for me at one time—and occasionally still is—to be really listened to by another person who did not give me easy answers and who truly valued me as a person. I have also gained a healthy control over my emotions as I learned to identify my beliefs that made me upset myself. Encounter groups also helped me experience the give-and-take of relationships on an intense personal level, seeing myself through the eyes of others, and seeing others through their own eyes.

Perhaps in these various journeys I was, at first, looking for some easy way to understand and work with people as a pastor, as well as an easy way to understand myself. I came to realize rather early, however, that no easy and simplistic approaches are effective for the pastor; nor for anyone else. Simplistic approaches to understanding and working with persons are inadequate because they tend to be deductive. Too often they work toward reducing the meaning of human experience rather than expanding it, and thereby the fullness of experience is neither captured nor adequately dealt with. It was through my study with Paul Johnson that I came to see the desirability of moving toward an expanding, rather than a receding field of perception and meaning; let each approach to understanding people enrich the work of the pastor, but let no one approach encapsulate that work into a rigid way of seeing and relating to persons.

So, although I came to appreciate many aspects of these various approaches to understanding and working with persons, I believe a holistic approach is needed. In order to be effective, we must utilize a holistic approach that includes spirituality, so that we may truly meet people at the center of their vital awareness. Only in this way can we help persons become fully human.

THE GESTALT PERSPECTIVE

Gestalt has proven invaluable in helping me move toward being a "physician of the soul," providing a holistic perspective for understanding myself and others. It is an approach to human experience that is inductive, providing a perspective that can help direct us to the path that leads toward claiming our spirituality.

The Gestalt approach had its inception in the work of Frederick S. Perls (1894-1970). "Fritz," as he was known to everyone, was trained professionally as a physician, psychoanalyst, and training analyst in the Freudian tradition. He practiced for a number of years as a psychoanalytically-oriented psychiatrist, but he eventually abandoned the psychoanalytic approach and the sexual theories of Freud and developed new theories and practices. He called his approach Gestalt, appropriating the rich meaning of that German word which has to do with wholeness. Life, said Fritz, consists of ongoing gestalts which continually form, reach completion, and recede for the next emerging gestalt. Life naturally contains a spontaneous flow and moves toward its own completion. It is only when our gestalts are not allowed to move to completion that life loses meaning and vitality, that we become neurotic and psychotic.

In the late 1930s and early 1940s Fritz began to articulate his new theories which were published in his first book, *Ego, Hunger, and Aggression*.[4] The term "Gestalt Therapy" was used as the title of a book written in collaboration with Ralph Hefferline and Paul A. Goodman, both of New York City.[5] As time went on there was an increasing tendency to refer to Perls' work as "The Gestalt Approach" rather than "Gestalt Therapy" because it has often been seen as an approach to personal growth and wholeness, rather than only a way to treat the sick. We are currently seeing an increasing proliferation of articles and books about the Gestalt approach as the experience and thinking of Gestaltists accumulates.[6]

Fritz stepped back, as it were, from the focus of the Freudian perspective, and took a broad look at the total life experience. Influenced by earlier contacts with Gestalt psychology under Kurt Goldstein at the Frankfurt Neurological Institute, and by existentialists like Martin Buber and Paul Tillich, Fritz began to formulate his view of human experience. He took into consideration the common observation that there is a natural flow to life, a spontaneous meaning that emerges as life is actually lived, and that the meaning of life is found more through living fully in the present than by rehashing the past.

From the Gestalt perspective, individual life experiences are seen most clearly as organism/environment structures. *Contact* between the individual (*organism*) and its situation (*environment*) provides the necessary experience for *assimilation, differentiation,* and *growth.* This contact comes by the focusing of a *figure* of interest against the *ground* of the organism/environment field. This is a dynamic interaction that produces *awareness.* Awareness is a natural occurrence as the organism becomes attentive to a point of contact where a *transaction* is taking place. Awareness allows for spontaneous and innovative *expressiveness* which, in turn, if the necessary fulfillment takes place, produces *closure* and completes the gestalt. This is a continually ongoing process. Fritz proposed the following equation to express this process:

ATTENTION = AWARENESS = EXPRESSIVENESS = CLOSURE

One of the simplest illustrations of a completed gestalt would be in relation to hunger. As the individual's attention is drawn inward, there is an awareness of certain physical sensations which are recognized as hunger. The body responds with appropriate food-seeking activity. As the body receives food, the need is satisfied and closure comes. The person is no longer hungry. Another awareness emerges, perhaps the need for sleep, etc.

If all our experiences continued in this way, life would be completely fulfilling and satisfying. The natural cycle of contact/withdrawal is, in reality, complicated at many points. Awareness can be a particular problem for so many of us who actually make little use of our senses. Sight and hearing are perhaps most frequently used in our attempts to become aware of what is around us, but too many of us have isolated ourselves from our other senses so that we are largely cut off from these avenues of our vital awareness. Even sight and hearing may be severely limited so that, as the scripture says, seeing we do not see and hearing we do not hear (Mark 8:18). To this we might add that far too often we taste but do not taste, smell but do not smell, and touch but do not feel. In our society we tend to downplay the body and refuse to let it share its wisdom with us or, more correctly, we deny this part of ourselves.

From the Gestalt perspective, we are seen as relying too heavily on our minds—our "computers" in Gestalt jargon—and often refusing to acknowledge input from our senses. This, from the perspective of the Gestalt approach, is far too characteristic of contemporary life, and the consequences are seen in the unhappy and fractured lives of so many people today.

Of course, even if we utilize our full awareness, gestalt completion may be blocked either by the individual or by circumstances. In relation to the illustration above, that of the satisfaction of hunger, let's assume that a person has become fully aware of hunger but there is nothing to eat. If this gestalt is not completed it will continue to seek completion; and the more acute the hunger becomes the more this need will become dominant in the organism/environment field. It may eventually result in actions that the person might not consider appropriate in other circumstances, as when David ate the holy bread from the altar (I Sam. 21:1-6). Only when the bread was eaten and the hunger receded, only when the gestalt was complete, could the next emerging gestalt become the focus of awareness.

Incomplete gestalts, often referred to in the Gestalt approach as *unfinished business,* whatever their cause, tend to repeatedly seek completion, but are unsuccessful because they are blinded by their own incompleteness. This results in frustration, unhappiness, incompleteness, sickness, and neurotic behavior. It may even be manifested in the extreme forms of pathological behavior, which we call mental illness.

Unfinished business must be finished if life is to have a normal flow. Unfinished business can arise in interpersonal relationships as well as in the way we meet, or do not meet, the needs of our own body. Unmet or aborted psychological and spiritual needs also may result in unfinished business. A love affair that ended abruptly and that had no closure, the need to say good-bye to something or someone we love, the denied need to move our bodies in simple exercise, or even to curse or bless God can all create unfinished business. Unless such gestalts are allowed to flow to completion, our lives become less than they could be and we too readily become miserable and ineffective.

It was this perspective that Fritz developed after immigrating to the United States in the late 1940s. I am convinced that we have a great deal to learn from him, although some in the religious field might question this because he acknowledged no formal religious commitment. Still, there is a growing recognition of the deep spirituality inherent in Perls' work. Naranjo, for example, has astutely commented that Fritz's spirituality is disguised, but no less real. Fritz deplored sham and pretense and sacrosanct beliefs that blocked personal authenticity and authentic encounter.[7] We miss the spiritual nature of Gestalt, also, if we are not aware that Fritz utilized a rather distinctive vocabulary. Where many today use such words as Higher Self, and others use the words soul or spirit, Fritz used the word organism. This use of such common or simple scientific words, did not require a belief system for one to understand his meaning. At times, this has tended to make the Gestalt approach appear simplistic thus obscuring the great heights and depths of Fritz's thinking and thereby also obscuring its spiritual nature.

GESTALT AND CHRISTIAN PERSPECTIVES

The Gestalt approach has a very important contribution to make to our spiritual life. Its theory offers a fresh perspective on the human spirit, and its process is capable of promoting spiritual growth.

For our purposes, we will consider the words *soul* and *spirit* to be synonymous. Biblical authorities are by no means unanimous on this matter, but there does seem to be considerable agreement that a lack of consistency exists in the way these words are used in the biblical material. In the Old Testament, for example, the words *soul, spirit,* and *heart* seem to be used with the same meaning at times, but with different meanings at other times. However, scholars do point to an underlying agreement in a basic concept of these words as they appear in the Old Testament. That concept is that there are two inseparable elements in human nature—physical and psychical. A similar situation exists in the New Testament. At times Paul tends to use the Hebrew understanding, at other times he does not. Jesus taught the indestructibility of the soul as the nonphysical aspect of life, while retaining a holistic perspective.[8]

Therefore, although some variance may occur in terminology in the biblical material, there seems to be a basic agreement in seeing human nature as (1) consisting of psychical and physical elements, and (2) that these two elements are inseparable. Here it may be noted that Perls strongly emphasized our unitary nature, denying that there was any separation between the mental and the physical.

In the biblical perspective the individual is seen in holistic terms. The individual was created a living *nephesh,* a living soul or spirit. The individual is seen as *being* a soul or spirit—not *having* one. This concept was basic to the life and culture of ancient Israel.

James Lynwood Walker suggests that the soul may appropriately be defined as "the center of the personality." He suggests that the Gestalt approach provides an avenue for giving substance to that definition since, in its holistic view, it helps us get in touch with our emotions, our feelings, our spirit.[9] It moves us at the vital center of our being, that point which was referred to in ancient Israel as the soul.

The creation story of Genesis, Chapters 2 and 3, sets forth the holistic view of persons. The key verse is Genesis 2:7 (KJV), "Then the Lord God formed man of dust from the ground, and breathed into his nostrils the breath of life, and man became a living nephesh."

Thus we are body and soul. In this ancient Hebrew idea there is no implication of dichotomy. It is a statement of our unity. The image of God is also seen as reflected in both body and soul in a unitary way. We are living beings because we have the breath of life. The physical body is a living soul because it is inspirited with the Creator's life-giving breath. Apart from breath there can be no life. The essence of our soulfulness is the quality of vitality, power, and aliveness within our human experience.

Our nature is grounded, of the earth. The theme of Genesis Chapter 2 is that of *adam-adamah* (man-earth). Here is a profound statement of the ecological unity we have with the environment, a unity too often forgotten today. Biblical scholars point to the association, in biblical materials, of our very being with the earth. It is perhaps not an overstatement to say that much of popular Christianity today has lost this conception of our grounded being. The emphasis is too often placed upon the Christian's connection to heaven, rather than to earth. This concept has its place, but inappropriately applied it tends to take us away from our groundedness in an earthly existence. (I cannot resist quoting the popular saying that "Some Christians are so heavenly minded they are no earthly good.")

The price of not being grounded is fragmentation, and it is primarily experienced by the individual as the inability to be alone, a nagging sense of incompleteness in life, and an unending search for things to fill the void of meaninglessness. We can neglect the reality of our intimate bond with the earth only at the peril of losing our vitality, our spirit. One of our needs today is to reclaim our bodies and our very real connection to the earth. Dietrich Bonhoeffer stated it very clearly and succinctly: "Escape from the body is escape from the spirit as well. Body is the existence-form of spirit, and spirit is the existence-form of body."[10]

It is at this point that the Gestalt approach has an important contribution to make to religion, for its basic thrust is to bring us to a full awareness of ourselves. It does this by helping us become aware of who we are as complete beings who experience our bodies fully. It helps us to ground ourselves in the reality of our experience by helping us to claim, and to be responsible for, our feelings, our emotions, and our vitality. It allows us to move toward closure in relation to our organic needs and helps us to embrace our own unique harmony with our environment, even fully experiencing the ground beneath our feet.

As we move closer to actualizing our human potential we become more fully a part of the vital ongoing process of creation. We, as part of creation, become whole when we appropriate the power of our unitary nature. From a theological perspective we might say that the fall comes and sin enters in when we move away from our ecological unity with our environment and begin living primarily in our heads. When this happens Gestaltists say we need "to lose our minds and come to our senses," that is, we need to move toward more holistic functioning in order to claim our full potential.

We are fully human only when we are whole beings, complete gestalts. We become a lively figure against the ground of our being when we can flow as a unity of volition, intention, and action. It is instructive to note that ancient Israel had no separate word for *will* such as we have today. The individual was seen as a being who was the totality of experienced needs, urges, instincts, and perceptions. Thinking was not seen as existing in objective and subjective modes. Thinking implied immediate, direct action, not simply abstraction. Even memory carried an immediacy and was linked to present action.

This same holistic approach to life was also integral to the life and ministry of Jesus. One point at which this is clearly illustrated is at the Last Supper (Matt. 26:17-29). Here the commemoration of His life takes place through participatory acts, the breaking of bread and the drinking from the cup, thereby transcending mere thought or words alone.[11] This type of full sensory experience brings a more complete awareness rather than relegating experience to a simple "head trip." Here again we see a startling similarity to the Gestalt approach, which urges us to "turn off our computers" and begin to enter experience in a holistic way.

At the core of the holistic life experience is the *self* or spirit. The theologian John B. Cobb Jr. argues that the pastor must have this spirit at the focus of all pastoral care and counseling. He says that the spirit *is* the self, it is the center of psychic life, and that, "One may 'use' one's reason, or 'control' one's emotions. One *is* one's self or spirit."[12]

There is need for careful definition in regard to the nature of self. Much of modern psychology and counseling—though not all—would say that the self is the sum total of the emotions, the body, the intellect, the ego, etc., but not more than this. The Christian perspective, says Cobb, is that self transcends these components individually and collectively. The self is spirit. This is an identical perception to the Gestalt approach, as we shall see in the chapter of this book titled "Peeling the Onion."

Thus, spiritual growth means striving for a wholeness that centers in spirit. This orientation will, by its very nature, inform all pastoral work. It will not mean abandoning current psychological or counseling knowledge. Instead, such knowledge will be embraced as a source of enhancement for wholeness in spirit.

One of the implications in this understanding of spiritual growth is that the personal self, or what is usually called ego, must be transcended if growth is to occur. Growth toward wholeness occurs only as we move beyond the personal self toward what today is being called the *transpersonal* or the *superconscious,* terms which carry the same meaning as *spiritual.* This is the pathway that leads to union with God in the Christian perspective.

It is encouraging that modern psychology and counseling, which for so long has focused almost exclusively on ego as the center of self-identification, have recently shown a vital interest in the transpersonal area. Notable examples may be seen in the work of Roberto Assagioli and his Psycho synthesis; Robert Girard and his Integral Psychology; and in what quite recently has been referred to as Transpersonal Gestalt.[13]

This new interest can certainly be applauded by pastors who, quite rightly, saw the limitation of much of modern psychology and counseling that focused mainly on personality adjustment or good mental health. We, as pastors, can never be content working with people on only such limited goals, as important as these goals are. The pastor is always concerned with the need for spiritual growth.

It is interesting to note that the concept of the transcendence of ego (usually referred to as self-transcendence) is a basic given in the East. Buddhism reflects this view as well as Yoga. Usharbudh Arya, for example, points out that yoga moves toward *dispassion,* where the self is no longer controlled by the passions, no longer restricted by such identifications and limitations.[14]

Within the Christian tradition we find the same emphasis. In the mystical tradition, for example, the unnamed author of *The Cloud of Unknowing* writes, "Every man has plenty of cause for sorrow but he alone understands the deep universal reason for sorrow who experiences that he is."[15] This is a statement of the vast superiority of life in the spirit. Once life in the spirit has been glimpsed, the old identifications of self can seem only the greatest sorrow by comparison.

The path of spiritual growth is not an easy one. It takes work and discipline. We do not easily give up identifications, we do not easily move beyond passions, and a danger lurks here. Not identifying with aspects of our psychic life can result in a denial of responsibility for them. But, as Cobb contends rightly, from the Christian perspective this would be an obvious error; the purpose of disidentification is to lead people to a more radical responsibility.

Here, then, lies the key to appropriate and effective pastoral care and counseling. This is a starting point for its distinctiveness, a recognition of, and response to, life in the spirit. Helping people achieve this life is the basic task of pastoral care.

PASTORAL CARE—AN ILLUSTRATION

Let us take a look at the illustration given by Cobb in regard to how the Christian understanding of spirit may influence pastoral care.[16]

Chester Carter and his wife moved into town. Chester joined the church but his wife did not. The pastor visited them in their home and Mrs. Carter simply stated she was not a church-going person.

The pastor, Jones, heard that Chester was in the hospital and went to visit him. He knew Chester was fifty-five years old, had three grown children, and that he worked for a large insurance company as an accounting clerk. Pastor Jones was a little surprised when Chester said that he had intended to make an appointment to see him. With little prompting Chester talked about many of his fears about work and his inability to get along with his male bosses. He stated that he had had many jobs over the years and very much wanted to keep his present job. He also revealed that he was very much attracted to the younger women in the office.

When the pastor returned to see Chester the next day he encouraged Chester to talk more about his situation. According to Chester, his primary concern seemed to be his strong attraction to the young women in the office. He also shared that he had fantasies about having romantic affairs with them. He admitted being repelled by his wife, as well as other women his own age. Yet, he was extremely ambivalent about relationships with younger women as he feared rejection. Chester also talked about a very difficult home life as a child, about a mother who beat him at times, and a father he never felt close to. He had few friends during his school years. He talked about his relationship with his wife as being quite unsatisfactory and as always "on the verge of divorce." Their sex life was far from satisfactory, and he confessed to impotence.

Pastor Jones clearly identified a number of psychological problems. But what could he do about them? He finally decided that the best thing he could do would be to make a referral. He did this and Chester joined a therapy group.

Cobb commends Pastor Jones for what he did for Chester. He visited him in the hospital in his role as pastor and he communicated openness and concern as evidenced by the sharing that Chester did. But beyond this Cobb says not much was distinctive about the relationship offered by the pastor. Taking Chester's verbalized concerns about the need to be able to enter relationships more freely with women, and the need for less fear of male superiors, the pastor arranged for these needs to be met—in this case by referral to a therapy group. This, Cobb says, was certainly appropriate from a Christian perspective.

Yet Cobb suggests that Christianity really does, or should, go a step beyond this by challenging our definition of needs. Although the preaching of Pastor Jones probably reflected this challenge, it did not seem to enter into this immediate pastoral relationship.

What more might Pastor Jones have done? Cobb suggests that the pastor might have attempted to use this situation to help Chester enter into spiritual existence. In this specific situation Cobb says that the pastor would not only have taken Chester's expressed desires seriously—the desire to get along better with male superiors and the desire to enter into intimate relations with women—but that the pastor could have addressed Chester's wish to be a different kind of person with different desires. He might have supported and encouraged this, bringing it more fully into consciousness and strengthening it.

Was there any reason to think that such aspirations might have been present in Chester? One indication seems to have been that Chester had joined the church, even when his wife did not. Surely this must have hinted at some kind of aspiration. What was the aspiration being expressed? How could it be nourished? When Chester was struggling with the real personal difficulties in his life, did it count for nothing? But let us suppose that the pastor does not have the expertise to help Chester with his psychological problems. Is the pastor to be satisfied with this? Cobb's answer is no, Chester still needed to see himself and his life in a wider perspective. He needed to be alerted to the dangers of self-preoccupation. Could it not even be possible, Cobb suggests, that a very real movement outward toward helping others in Christian service might do as much for Chester's "problems" as group therapy? Service to others offers the possibility of promoting self-transcendence in such a way that a person need no longer be under the control of "problems."

At this point I want to let stand the questions raised by Cobb. In the last chapter of this book, "Where the Rubber Hits the Road," I will give an example of how a Gestalt approach might help a pastor who is assisting individuals to achieve spiritual growth. However, before that can be done, I think it is necessary to gain a more complete understanding of the Gestalt approach. How does Gestalt see the total life experience? What is the theoretical base that undergirds the Gestalt perspective? How do pastors experience Gestalt work when they are recipients of it as part of a growth process? Only when such questions as these are addressed will we be ready to gain a clear figure/ground formation in relation to the application to pastoral care.

Chapter 2

Becoming Fully Human

In the last chapter we discussed the task of helping people live life in the spirit as the goal of pastoral care and counseling, noting that this could only happen as people were helped to be fully human. We now turn to examining the theme of being fully human.

The Gestalt approach focuses on the spontaneous and full experiencing of the ebb-and-flow of life; on living synchronously with life as it is and entering fully into the life experience. Some time ago there was a popular song which, echoing Ecclesiastes 3:1-8, contained the lyric, "There is a time for everything under the sun." This might well be the theme song of the Gestalt approach. The underlying theme of the song was awareness and expressiveness, and the chorus echoed the importance of contact, withdrawal, freedom, and responsibility—each emerging gestalt moving toward closure and an expanding apprehension of life in the spirit.

To become fully human means that we take our experience seriously. In fact, Gestaltists insist that experience must be given first priority as we seek to become fully human. Currently, there is such a strong emphasis placed on the understanding of our human experience that the understanding of experience has been seen as more important than the experience itself. This tendency has been due in large part, though not exclusively, to the influence of psychoanalysis; the emphasis on the interpretation of experiences in one's life seems to take on a greater importance than the actual experiences themselves. This has led to a devaluing of experience and a tendency for people "to live in their heads," thus blocking the holistic experience. The result is certainly that we become less than fully human. This same phenomenon can also be seen in regard to religion. When the intellectual search for meaning in religious experience—as reflected in systematic theology, for example—becomes of more importance than religious experience itself, then the result is a truncating of our humanity.

In this regard, it is instructive to look at the life of Jesus. What is especially obvious in the Gospel account of His life is that He did not simply sit around preaching sermons about the meaning of life, nor did He theologize much about it. Rather, He entered fully into all aspects of life and relationships with others to the point that the more fastidious religionists of His day called Him a "winebibber and a sinner" (Matt. 11:19, KJV). It was only some considerable time after His death that people began to talk about the "meaning" of His life, eventually producing a large body of theology that far too often has become more important than His actual life. Early Christianity, however, thought of itself as "a way of life."

The tendency to abstract meaning about life experience in a way that detracts from the experience itself is often referred to as *aboutism*. People will often be heard saying, "Let me tell you about my problem." These words betray, or more correctly identify, the process that is taking place. Rather than concentrating directly on the problem, this person is actually deflecting such concentration by intellectual processing. The Gestaltist would insist that it is the actual experience that is of primary importance, and that talking about it will usually be of little help. It is an all too common observation that a person can apparently resolve something on an intellectual level without changing anything on a behavioral level.

Because of this aversion to aboutism there has been a popular misconception that Gestalt has no interest in making any rational or intellectual sense. This is certainly not the case. In fact, the vast Gestalt literature that has developed over the last two or three decades at the close of the twentieth century stands as clear evidence of serious intellectual activity in this field.[1] As we shall see in the next chapter, it is more a matter of setting intellectual activity in proper perspective and of not allowing it to be confused with experience. If the time comes when Gestalt theory is seen as more important than experience, then Gestalt will have forsaken its own birthright. As a Gestaltist works with another person in a helping relationship, it is the actual immediate experience that is the focus of attention. It is for this reason, as well as the fact that the Gestalt approach isn't usually used with the mentally ill, that Gestaltists rarely speak about diagnosis. While many Gestaltists, such as the Polsters, have clearly identified and described the theory and practice of Gestalt, such work is done only as perspective on living experience and not for the purpose of providing a diagnostic system.[2] Unless a label can help us to really understand another person better, and hence be a help to them, it may simply dehumanize the person. Labeling is also very problematic because it tends to assume that we, as counselors, know what a person's experience really means to them. For these reasons, Gestaltists tend to shy away from diagnoses.

The Gestalt stance implies that it is the person who interprets his or her own behavior, not the counselor. What a given behavior may mean to the counselor, or what it has meant to a thousand other people, does not take precedent over its meaning to the individual who experiences it.

In order to understand our behavior and our life experience, we must put experience before mere formulations of it. Understanding the meaning of an event in our life experience requires more than simply making intellectual formulations in regard to it. What is required is that we allow ourselves to fully experience it in the present moment. Knowing is a quality of full experiencing. It includes rational processing and full sensory experiencing. When this is a full and complete process, the meaning is present as a part of the process and not simply something abstracted from it or tacked onto it. This is an expanded understanding of meaning, removed from the simplicity of mere intellectualizing. It parallels the biblical perspective that says we are body and soul and function in a unitary and holistic way.

HOW WE BLOCK OUR EXPERIENCE

The Gestaltist is not much concerned with explanations of unconscious processes, but is rather pragmatic in outlook. Perls took the position that the unconscious was, by definition, unknowable. Only immediate behavior, including rational behavior, can be dealt with. This is not to be taken as a kind of psychological naiveté. We will remember that Perls had the highest credentials as a psychoanalyst and was thoroughly familiar with a wide variety of theories and perspectives regarding the unconscious. It was against this background and his attendant experience as a psychiatrist and psychoanalyst that Perls developed a different perspective. He observed that if something is unconscious, then it is thereby not in consciousness and in terms of present reality has no vitality. It is part of the ground of our experience against which the figure of our present experience stands. It is this figure, this emerging Gestalt, that is the focus of our attention.

As Perls looked at human experience, he noted four primary ways in which we block ourselves from the fullness of our own experience. These he called (1) projection, (2) introjection, (3) retroflection, and (4) confluence. Projection and introjection were lifted straight out of psychoanalysis.

Projection

We may note that we are often faced with paradoxes and inconsistencies in how we perceive the world outside ourselves. Our experience often shows us that people see quite different things in the same environment. In a very real sense, each one of us creates our own world. No one knows, for example, what color is really like. We do know that our sense receptors, the eyes, seem to react similarly to it and we are able to talk with other people about color in meaningful ways. But what is "out there" we have no direct way of knowing. So each of us *projects* our meaning onto it. To a great degree, this is very helpful and even necessary in daily life. However, if our projections are confused with what is "out there," we block ourselves from ever gaining a clear understanding of it.

This has important implications for self-understanding. If we are to flow spontaneously with life, we must try to see things as they are, and not merely see what we want to see. We also must see ourselves as we are. This is easier said than done. In intrapersonal terms it requires a kind of honesty about ourselves that can be excruciatingly difficult to face. The biblical story of Adam and Eve (Genesis 3:1-13) gives us a classic instance of projection. Adam projects blame on Eve for his actions saying, "The woman thou gavest me, she gave me of the tree . . . ," and Eve projects blame onto the serpent saying, "The serpent beguiled me. . . ."

When we project we refuse to take responsibility and thus block ourselves, our awareness, our vitality and, in biblical terms, we *fall* from what we are and might become. Projection is always a subtle process; it is difficult for us to recognize it when it pertains to *our* behavior. Like the serpent, it slithers around, hardly visible at times but, nevertheless, it is very real and powerful.

In *Gestalt Therapy* Perls spoke of the sexually inhibited woman who continually complained that men were making improper advances toward her as an example of projection.[3] Unable to claim her own sexuality in a healthy way, she could only see it in others. Paradoxically, this cut her off from healthy sexual contact with men and made her life miserable. Projection is a subtle serpent purveying inedible fruit.

Introjection

The Gestalt approach, with its emphasis on the present, in no way denies that we are what we are because of our past. However, Gestaltists would say that it is more a matter of how we allow what we have taken in to affect our present life. Some things we take in—like healthy food or life-giving interpersonal experience—can provide a rich ground for living a vital life. However, at times we may take in much that is not life giving or nutritious for either body or soul. If we reach out toward life on the basis of what is unhealthy in us, we need not be surprised if our attempts to do so often seem to be self-defeating. Things which are taken in but cannot be assimilated because they are antagonistic to the individual's life are called *introjects*. One Gestaltist used an apt illustration, referring to them as sandwiches in plastic bags. They are encapsulated in such a way that they become a lump in the stomach rather than providing nutrition.

In a way, introjection is the reverse of projection. Rather than placing appropriate meaning on experience, one accepts an erroneous view from outside experience and acts as though it were true.

The pastor is by no means immune to this process. As people leave the church on Sunday morning they say things like, "You're the best preacher I've ever heard!" or "No one has ever preached the Gospel like you just did." So the pastor may begin to believe that this is really true. Critical judgment is set aside. These comments are taken in as absolute truth and the pastor begins to think and act accordingly. Reasons may be invented for confirming that what was said is really true. A false identity is built up and plays against the true nature of the pastor's experience. Certainly no ministry can endure for long on the basis of such false identity.

In many ways introjection may even be subtler than projection. We take in, for example, many attitudes and values from what we believe are important and reliable sources—our parents, our schools, even our churches. How difficult it is to be able to discriminate between what really fits us and what does not. Even an attitude or value that served us well at one time may work against us at another. To dislodge an introject will often take a lot of work, a lot of risk and courage. Even being able to identify it may be very difficult. It is often difficult to differentiate our identifications with others from introjects. Identifications are models we use as guides that give directions in our lives. Introjects are parts of other people's characters that we take in "hook, line, and sinker" as our own.

I have often thought that a great deal of the ministry of Jesus might be seen as helping people recognize and dislodge introjects—things that people have taken in, but which really did not fit the reality of their life experience. Many times he said, "Ye have heard it was said by them of old time . . . But I say unto you . . ." (Matt. 5:21, 22, KJV). We must always be open to looking critically at what we assume about ourselves and the world if our lives are to be lived in fullness and if truth is not to be truncated.

Retroflection

As the word implies, the process of retroflection means the turning of energy inward. This appears to be a word that Fritz used to describe what Freud called reversal. In addition, Fritz also uses it to explain what Freud called repression, reaction formation, undoing, displacement, and most all of the other defense mechanisms Freud described. Perls probably made retroflection so inclusive because he was aware that retroflection had, at a deeper level, something in common with all these defenses. Fritz was a master of simplification and exposing the obvious.

In retroflecting it is as though the person, unsuccessful in relating to the outside world, energy internalizes that same, either physically or psychologically, or both. Psychosomatic illnesses, for example, may be seen as the outcome of retroflective process. Van De Riet and colleagues give an illustration of this when they note that a client gave a report of a burning sensation in the left rib cage, as if it had been bruised.[4] When, in the process of counseling, the client was asked who he would like to bruise in his family, he indicates who this person is but also says that he is afraid to express his anger. The energy, therefore, that should have gone out toward the other person, was turned inward. Needless to say, prolonged retroflection can lead to illnesses if not undone. The client mentioned here, for example, might well have had to consult a physician for the treatment of an ulcer at a later time had he not dealt with his anger in a healthy way.

The undoing of a retroflection, in other words, reversing the energy, is a life-giving process. It also involves a good deal of risk. Unleashed anger, for instance, can easily lead to inappropriate actions if not processed carefully. Thus, Gestaltists utilize the encounter between themselves and the retroflection in such a way so as to provide a safe environment, where the release of energy can be controlled. There is always a certain amount of rebellion involved in undoing a retroflection, thus necessitating the control. The result, however, of appropriate release of energy, is that it allows life energy to flow out in more spontaneous and less self-defeating ways. Energy becomes constructive rather than destructive.

Confluence

Confluence basically refers to a lack of awareness or definition of self. In the Gestalt perspective, healthy contact with the environment involves awareness and excitement. When this healthy contact is blocked, the effect is often an unawareness of what is taking place. Things begin to blur together and no clear figure emerges. We may not be sure just where the boundaries are between ourselves and another person, or what we may want or need at a given time. The excitement of life is lost; we are out of touch with our spirit, our soul. We may have little sense of self or "I." This is nowhere more clearly illustrated than with the infant who, in the first three to six months of life, is confluent with its mother. The infant does not have a clear distinction between self and mother; they are experienced as one. In the first steps of differentiation, figure takes the quality of all or extremes, and ground the quality of nonexistence. Thus, whatever exists, exists in its extreme form, or not at all. As confluence gives way, this splitting dissolves and relative degrees of existences are applied to situations and experiences which are differentiated. The developmental experience, if it proceeds normally, gradually allows the infant to gain a sense of "I" and "not I," as the confluency is gradually broken. Adult life is characterized by clear differentiation of self

Yet, there is a place for confluence in spiritual life. We cannot understand many of the contradictions in the universe. One contradiction is that it takes confluence, or oneness, with God and the universe to contact the spirit within us. However, it takes definition and differentiation to make use of what is contacted and received. Truly living life in the spirit comes through the claiming of individuality, as Jesus did, rather than putting that individuality aside. Too often, we believe that putting the needs of others first means that we must deny our individuality. From a Gestalt perspective, such a stance would be an unhealthy confluency. We will do well to remember that Jesus said we are to, "love our neighbors as we love ourselves"(Matt. 22:39), not *instead* of ourselves. We do disservice to ourselves as well as to others when we deny our own individuality and our own personal needs. Such confluency robs everyone of their vitality. It is also interesting to note that we have a great deal to learn about ourselves by observing how we treat our neighbors. Treating our neighbor well or badly is, basically, a reflection of how we treat ourselves. Even though we treat our neighbors badly, we undoubtedly are loving them as ourselves.

An illustration of the life-denying nature of confluency can often be found in marriage. In many traditional marriages the wife has often repressed her own individuality and merged her life into that of her husband and children. At one time I did considerable marriage counseling in a church clinic. From that experience I became aware of the destructive force of such confluency. I found that a large percentage of the wives who came for counseling were struggling to break out of confluent relationships that were destroying both themselves and their families. For years the wife had gone along with whatever the husband wanted to do and had always "done what was best for the children." She had not given consideration to herself as an individual; she had perhaps even considered it sinful to do so. Why, then, having lived an exemplary life, was she so unhappy? Why did there seem to exist a subtle force that was destroying the family? Every awareness, however fleeting, of her own needs brought on feelings of guilt which, in turn, brought on feelings of resentment toward the husband. The husband also responded with guilt and resentment, and he was angry that the wife did not appreciate all that he had been trying to do for her. The children were likewise enmeshed in this vicious circle. How is it possible to break out of it? The Gestaltist would say that the only way to break such confluency is by attending to our needs, articulating them, discovering our own directions, and honoring them. This is always a difficult struggle. Some marriages can survive necessary restructuring, others cannot.

Confluency is one of the four ways we block ourselves from fullness of our own experiences. Confluency differs from the three others mentioned in that it can operate as a complete system to block awareness, whereas the other three are interdependent. Confluence, in its purest, primitive form, can survive without projection, introjection, or retroflection. This, however, rarely occurs except in severely psychotic children. Projection, introjection, retroflection, and confluence do not operate in isolation from one another in the average person seen in pastoral counseling. They are, in life experience, both interlocking and functionally interrelated. Projected identification, for example, is a combination of confluency, projection, and introjection between two persons where each (in a confluent manner, and through projection and introjection) trades parts of themselves that the other member of the pair does not mind adopting. Thus, a passive woman who cannot stand her spurts of aggression or anger marries a man who cannot stand his occasional feelings of passivity. He then becomes completely macho and adopts her aggression. She becomes more passive, adopting his passivity. They project onto each other a part of themselves they cannot stand but which the other partner is comfortable with, or can take pride in. When the individual no longer blocks functioning in these ways, that individual becomes more fully human.

Fritz Perls focused on dealing primarily with the organism's needs and how it those needs were fulfilled. He stressed the concept of responsibility and how closure is made or blocked—or prematurely made—on developmental levels in growth and development. Projection, introjection, and retroflection prevent gestalt closure problems at various development levels, according to Fritz. Confluency was seen by him as another interference with developmental closure, but he died before he could explore this area in depth. However, the work he did in this area hints at a whole new area of psychotherapy that may dwarf previous psychotherapy discoveries. Within this confluency are the roots of our origins—spiritual, biological, and psychological. Within this confluency, also, is a nondifferentiated self—a self which lacks boundaries and, when contacted, can cause such an expansive feeling that it may be impossible to feel any differentiation of the self. Herein lies the possibility of the deepest definition of the self or the deepest loss one can experience—a loss of self-knowledge. It is within this confluence that the most microscopic definitions of the self lie.

Formerly, this confluency was thought to be just an inner glob of chaos, symbiosis, or unbound energy and obliterated awareness. It is becoming increasingly obvious that it appeared that way because we were unable to see the extremely refined strands of identity which lie in confluency. The person having difficulty because of excessive confluency was meeting either global attitudes by others or his own hypersensitivity which lies within the confluency. The patient's difficulties detoured counselors and therapists, making it difficult for them to focus in on microscopic lines of identity.

What are these microscopic lines of identity within the confluence? I will summarize some.

There is a spectrum of differentiation which runs from bonding, at one end, and to you/me at the other end.[5] At the bonding end, everything that is soft is said to be one's self, and everything hard to be nonself, regardless of the origin of the experience. Pleasure and gratification are parts of the soft self. If the bonding experience is satisfactory, the center of awareness and the self are in the soft self. If it is unsatisfactory, a split occurs between the center of awareness and the self. In this split it is as if there is a soft, inner-self and a hard outer-self that is a nonself, like an egg with its eggshell. Life and the inanimate are experienced as "all inanimate."

At the interactional end of the confluence is a sharing of responses.[6] It is a two-person confluency in which sharing becomes the height of ecstasy at times. It is a mutual action and reaction, and the higher the degree of sharing, the greater the pleasure which eventually leads to ecstasy. Mature sexual behavior associated with love lies here. In between these two is mirroring. This is a confluency in which two persons mirror each other's behavior. It mostly occurs unconsciously.

An example of this in counseling is when the therapist misses an appointment and the client cancels the next appointment. Revenge is a mirroring and stems from confluency. Infatuation can be a type of mirroring, which can also lead to a type of ecstasy. This, in turn, may lead to an out-of-control confluency. Although the infatuated person is experiencing it as a two-person confluency, there really is only one active participant and the other person is, at times, completely ignorant of the infatuation. A person who constantly agrees with you is also exhibiting mirroring.

Attachment is somewhere between mirroring and the interactional end. Here, one person nurtures the dependent need of the second person. The first person has mature needs that are nurtured by the second person—such as the need to be a good parent or teacher. Helping the client to define his or her confluency lines leads to the definition of identity at the deepest level. The spectrum of confluency is diagrammed in Table 2.1.

Therapeutic postures are important in dealing with these different lines. They all may be present simultaneously or in altered sequence. More likely, the client who experiences confluency will proceed from left to right in the diagram, from any given starting point. If the confluent experience is a "Soft me—hard, not me," the proper therapeutic posture is soft. The level of trust here does not extend beyond trusting one's own behaviors. Often, because a client has not made closure on being able to trust his or her own behaviors, the client remains stuck at this level. Firmness may be needed at times, given in a most supportive manner.

The mirroring client needs an "ideal behaving" therapeutic posture. That is, the therapist needs to behave in the most ideal manner in terms of knowledge, honesty, consideration, cleverness, etc. to give the client a good mirror. Rudimentary trust may have been developed (i.e., trusting someone to pay you for your work) but a person as a whole is not trusted. There is little concept of loyalty or attachment.

The counselor must be careful not to mirror the patient, which may be difficult to avoid if the patient starts depreciating the counselor. The counselor must maintain a positive stance, not becoming defensive, if the mirroring behavior is discussed. The client needs to see it as a step to higher levels of differentiation of the self.

TABLE 2.1. The Spectrum of Confluency

Bonding	**Mirroring**	**Attachment**	**Interactional**
Confluency present and not recognized	Confluency unconsciously recognized	Confluency recognized dimly in consciousness	Hyperconscious of confluency and actively seeks out own identity

The client with an attachment confluency needs a nurturing, continued, accurate definition of the difference between what he needs and what the counselor needs. In this case, people may be trusted but the world or universe is not. The client's conception of God tends to be negative. Maintaining nurturing and contact with the client is important.

In the interactional confluence there is a hyperconsciousness. The client actively seeks to establish an identity. It is important for the counselor to recognize this goal and be practical/reactive but not hypersensitive/reactive to the patient's own hypersensitivity and disclosures. The concept of trust is developing in the direction of trusting mankind, the world, the universe, and God in a positive, whole manner. The client, as differentiation occurs, however, often expects the counselor to be immaturely judgmental and reactive to the hard truths about himself which were formerly hidden in confluency. The counselor needs to be wise, practical, levelheaded, and mature in his judgment and reactions. When the client feels unduly judged, the client needs to learn that he expects this because he judged himself in this immature manner while in confluency.

Spirituality emerges as a line of identity within all of the above mentioned spectrums of confluency. It only takes on a positive wholeness with a cohesive meaning as the interactional is met, and the person is finding identity in relationship to the universe.

Two additional lines of identity make their appearance in the confluency. They may surface in some hidden form and can require microscopic alertness, sensitivity, and differentiation to unravel. One is deep love for parents, family, and mankind hidden behind grandiosity, resentment, and revenge. This is one of the focuses of orthodox psychoanalysis.

In counseling, the client's identity lines need to be defined repeatedly at deeper and deeper levels.

HERE AND NOW

The cornerstone of the Gestalt approach is the here and now. The Gestalt approach seeks to promote awareness, making it possible for people to be more fully present. The Polsters have highlighted the importance of this perspective through the use of the phrase "power is in the present."[7] Although this statement may seem to be rather obvious, many people have difficulty appropriating this truth in the way that they live. While it is true that we are all, in large measure, what we are as a result of past experience, Gestaltists insist that we can only work on ourselves and our relationships in the present. Likewise, from the Gestalt perspective, it is just as impossible to deal with the future. We have only the *present*, only the here and now.

In fact, even time appears to be an illusion. Today, science tells us that other dimensions of the universe create the illusion of time, so that we do not really know what past or future are with any certainty. Additionally, certain spiritual experiences such as precognition and past-life experience, which are increasingly reported by our spiritual colleagues, recast our notions of past and future into a practical concept. Time may function as a law without being the ultimate truth. This I refer to as practical past and practical future.

In the Lord's Prayer, Jesus says, "Thy kingdom come. Thy will be done in earth, as it is in heaven" (Matt. 6:10, KJV). Here we see the word "come" (future) put together with "done" (past). Is Jesus giving us a Gestalt phrase, as Fritz might, to bring past and future into the now? If so, then the purpose of that part of the prayer is to bring the heaven awareness out of the past or future into the *now*—that is, to experience heaven on earth now, rather than living on illusions that rob the present moment of its vitality. Think what this does to our behavior. Living in heaven, here and now on earth! To live a now-life one must enter the present emerging Gestalt fully, whether it be a memory of the past, the need to eat, or planning for the future. The Gestaltist cautions, however, against deluding ourselves into thinking that we are someplace other than in the present.

In the Gestalt approach the important thing is to *concentrate* on the present moment. It is this concentration that assists in the completion of the emerging gestalt, producing awareness that leads to spontaneity, expressiveness, and closure. Any attempt to live in the past or future is only an illusory escape from making contact with the power of the present and living fully in the present moment.

Living fully in the present is not an easy thing to do. Much of today's popular attitudes and lifestyles do not take the present seriously. Even in church we are frequently admonished to "remember the past." The past, whether relating to the saints of the church or the heroes of the state, preoccupies our everyday lives. Religion has emphasized the commandments and teachings of antiquity that have presumably been given to us "for our own good." It also has emphasized the lives of the exemplars of all that is seen as good and holy in the past. The state reminds us to keep the laws and adhere to the ideals set for us by our forefathers. Strict penalties often await us if we stray and forget the past.

The future preoccupies us also. The Christian religion has put great emphasis on the kingdom of God and heaven. The present, we are often told, gains meaning only in relation to the future goal of reaching heaven. The state also reminds us of the future. We are told to work and plan for the future society, to stave off the present energy crisis, etc., and only by so doing can we fulfill the dreams of the past. We carry into the twenty-first century a continuing work ethic that claims the future for us.

It is not my intention here to denigrate hard work or future planning, but rather to simply point out how difficult it is to focus on the present moment in our society. This same difficulty may be seen in counseling. Counseling in general, including much of the pastoral counseling movement, has naturally reflected the society around it. The first half of the twentieth century saw a great preoccupation with the past in counseling. It was exemplified in the classical Freudian psychoanalytic method, which had a great influence on pastoral counseling. This approach did, indeed, make a distinctive contribution to that century and has had an influence that continues into the twenty-first century, but its emphasis is on the past.

In the latter half of the twentieth century, we saw a dramatic move to a different theoretical and operational perspective. At the forefront of this movement was Rogerian counseling. The movement included many apparently diverse systems ranging from encounter groups and sensitivity groups to a variety of counseling systems, including the Gestalt approach. Frank Goble referred to this movement as "The Third Force."[8] These new approaches to counseling and personal growth all have one important characteristic in common—they all put more emphasis on the present than on past or future. They also emphasize our freedom of choice rather than a behavioristic determinism that gives almost exclusive power to the past.

If power is in the present, how do we account for the apparent effectiveness of Freudian psychoanalysis, both in its classic and in its modified forms? While the Gestaltist would question the extent of the effectiveness of this system, it might also be noted that even such a past-oriented system encourages patients to deal with the present, even though this may not have been intended. We may take the psychoanalytic idea of transference and countertransference as a case in point. Freud saw the current patient-therapist relationship as a recapitulation of previous relationships, taking its power from the past. Yet, in actual practice, Freud put great emphasis on the present relationship between therapist and patient.

The Gestalt approach emphasizes that only the present exists now. This seems like a fatuously obvious statement, but we seem far from recognizing the implications of its truth, especially for personal growth. The result is the truncation of life that we call neurotic living. Gestaltists see this neuroticism as the direct result of an unwillingness to live in the present. Living has the potential to be a satisfying, growing experience, one that flows naturally from moment to moment without constraint. Claiming that potential is the very personal task for each one of us, a task to be taken up in the present moment. The more we succeed at this task, the more fully human we become.

Chapter 3

Peeling the Onion

This chapter discusses some of the techniques used in Gestalt therapy, as well as some of the activities that are often seen in Gestalt groups (referred to in Gestalt literature as the rules and games of the Gestalt approach). Perhaps this chapter should not be written. As I start to write it, I have a fantasy of Perls rising from his grave. He says, "Ward, how can you do this? You know Gestalt is not just a matter of techniques, gimmicks, explanations!"[1] I ponder his statement a bit, then I say, "But Fritz, you once wrote a chapter on the very same subject."[2] There is a trace of a smile on his face as my fantasy fades.

In talking about the attempt of many systems of psychotherapy to understand human personality, Perls once likened these approaches to peeling an onion. He said that they systematically peel off the layers of personality one by one, attempting to understand the *why* of each component of the psyche in order to come to an understanding of the person. But, Perls noted, if you peel off the layers of an onion one by one, what you are left with is not "the real onion," but rather with no onion at all! I think the same thing is true in regard to understanding how any counseling or therapeutic system operates. If we think we can really understand an approach by carefully identifying each premise, each technique, we are headed for disappointment. We end up with a collection of pieces. We can easily miss the larger Gestalt. The sum is more than the total of the parts.

As far as I know, there is no system of counseling or therapy that follows a rigid set of techniques, claiming that if they are adhered to rigidly the therapeutic result will always occur. Even in behavior therapy, where we might expect this to be true, it is not. Aubrey Yates, for example, notes that in behavior therapy, ". . . there are no standard techniques that can (or should) be employed in a routine fashion." Even here, ". . . each case represents a new problem, to be tackled in its own right."[3]

The Gestalt approach respects individuality and seeks to respond freely and creatively to it. It does not seek to develop a psychological theory in the strict sense of that word. Nor does it offer a methodology, a set of techniques that a counselor, pastoral or otherwise, may use and thus claim to be a Gestaltist. What is considered essential is that the gestalt of each life be respected; that each individual be seen in a holistic way, with the realization that no theory is capable of the total understanding of the individual and that no one technique will be helpful in every situation.

Yet, every counseling system does tend to function in certain generally identifiable ways. Some techniques are used more than others. As we attempt to understand a particular approach to a helping relationship, it is useful to look at some of the theories its adherents have enunciated, and to look at some of the techniques that have been employed. This will not be a problem as long as we do not allow our attention to be focused exclusively on these layers of the onion, rather than on the onion itself.

It will also be helpful, for perspective, to understand the theory of change that is inherent in the Gestalt approach. This has been referred to by Beisser as the paradoxical theory of change.[4] The Gestalt approach says that people change when they become what they are, rather than when they try to become something they are not.

From this perspective the Gestaltist does not try to change anyone. The Gestaltist encourages the person to be what that person is, on the premise that change does not occur by trying to be different. Only as the person stands firmly in present experience can any movement take place. This movement occurs in a spontaneous, holistic way when the person fully claims the present. Paradoxical!

Here again, we see the uniqueness of the Gestalt approach. Other systems would see change taking place quite differently. The psychoanalytically oriented therapist would use such devices as dream interpretation, free association, and the transference relationship to produce change. Reward or punishment for behavior would be used by the behavior therapist. By way of contrast, the Gestaltist assists the individual to focus more clearly on the present and to experience it to the fullest. *What* is being experienced? *How* is it being experienced? Is there unfinished business? What is seeking completion in the person's life? How is that completion being blocked? Can the person take responsibility for the blocking? It is the Gestaltist's task to help the individual become aware of the now, the present moment, and to fully experience the *what* and *how* of behavior in the now.

From the Gestalt perspective counseling may be seen as an art form. The Gestalt counselor is like an artist who works in a creative way. True, it is the experience of the counselee that is the focus of concentration. The artistry which takes place here is not that which occurs between an inanimate object and a living person, but between two living people. This encounter, to be productive, must be a genuine meeting of these two people, a meeting at the center of vital awareness. The stereotype of the aloof, uninvolved therapist is certainly out of place here. In this regard, Gestalt has much in common with other counseling approaches such as Rogerian counseling, which put a strong emphasis on the mutuality of the counselor/counselee relationship.

What the Gestaltist brings to the encounter is his or her own full humanness. The basic tool in this encounter is not a carefully worked-out system of diagnosis and treatment or a predetermined arsenal of techniques, but a human genuineness. It requires a spontaneity of encounter, a wisely moderated sharing of feeling, thought, and action. In a sense, "anything goes," but the "anything goes" is within the context of a highly appropriate, artistic response, rather than being a license for irresponsibility. It requires considerable training and personal integration on the part of the Gestaltist.

Now let's examine the rules, games, and resources of the Gestalt approach, keeping in mind that they do not represent a rigid kind of system. Instead, they can be seen as perspectives on an art form, examples of art work, which may enrich our ground of experience so that we may more clearly understand and appreciate the phenomenon of the Gestalt approach.

RULES

The Gestaltists have found that work with both individuals and groups seems to be most effective when certain rules, or guidelines, are followed. These rules may or may not be explained prior to a given session. Some Gestalt group facilitators will go over them before a session and allow for discussion; others will allow the rules to emerge in the session itself. Here again, there is no set rule. The introduction of the rules is done in more of an artistic than a standard way.

The Principle of the Now

The goal of Gestalt work is to promote awareness. The focus of awareness is *now*. The Gestaltist will use a variety of techniques to keep this focus. The Gestaltist might begin by asking a person, "What is your now?" or "What are you feeling right now?" The focus is always now. Most of us find that it is exceedingly difficult to stay in the now. We avoid the present by talking about the past, or by drifting off into fantasy. One task of the Gestaltist is to help the client become aware of the fact that they are drifting or fantasizing, or in some way avoiding the present. This does not mean, as was pointed out previously, that there is no interest in historical material. It does mean that historical material must be dealt with in a present context.

The Gestaltist also takes the view that the relationship between counselor and counselee is a real part of life and must be dealt with as a real *now* experience. The client involved in Gestalt counseling is very much living life in that process. Emphasis throughout Gestalt work remains on the now. Later in this chapter we will look at some of the techniques that may be used to help clients keep this focus.

I and Thou

The Gestaltist contends that if there is to be meaningful communication between people, there must be directness. The client might say, "People just don't like me" or "I guess I'm just angry at the world." Such statements are seen, from the Gestalt perspective, as avoidance of real contact with other persons. Fritz acknowledged his debt to Martin Buber, and others, for his emphasis on direct contact. Genuine contact occurs in the coming together of "I" and "Thou." There is no genuine contact when I talk "about" a relationship or when I talk "past" another person. However, if I look directly at another person, use the person's name, and share my thoughts, feelings, and then there is the possibility of true contact, real communication. As we shall see, Gestalt games are often designed to promote this direct type of communication.

No Gossiping

Another form of indirect communication is the way in which we talk about other persons who are present—perhaps interpreting some aspect of their behavior—while acting as though they were not present. This is called gossiping and is seen as blocking communication. The Gestaltist tries to help the client to correct this. For example, in a Gestalt group a client might talk about another group member to the group facilitator, saying something like, "John's problem is that he doesn't share anything personal in the group." The group facilitator might respond, "Say that again, only this time say it directly to John." This is far more than a simple quibble over semantics. It is a direct way in which "I" and "Thou" communication may be fostered and our business with the other person can be completed. It is the accumulation of such unfinished business that blocks spontaneous living and helps to stifle our own genuineness.

"It" and "I" Language

The Gestaltist believes that functioning can only be healthy if we claim our bodies and their actions. We tend to objectify our body or body parts, as though they were really not a part of ourselves. For example, the Gestaltist might ask a group member, "What is your eye doing?" The group member might respond, "It is winking." Whereupon the Gestaltist might suggest, "Can you say, *I* am winking?" While doing such a thing might seem a little ridiculous at first, it points out that we do seem to have trouble taking responsibility for our bodies; this split-off part of our experience needs integration.

Such a perspective allows for the non-rational wisdom of the total human organism. The communication of the nonrational aspect of the organism is seen as being of equal, if not greater, importance than the rational aspect. It is a wisdom that seldom seems subject to error in its assessment of the needs and aspirations of the total human organism. It is "organismic knowing." Therefore, the use of "I" and "It" language is one way to call attention to what is needed for holistic functioning.

Use of the Awareness Continuum

Since it is so important to allow for the wisdom of the total human organism, getting in touch with this wisdom calls for more than isolated or casual attempts at body awareness. Focusing on the body in a systematic way is important for getting in touch with a deeper understanding of our human experience, an understanding that must involve the total organism.

To promote this type of systematic awareness the Gestaltist may invoke what is called the awareness-continuum rule, which allows the total organism to speak. The Gestaltist might ask the person, "What are you aware of now?" After the person responds the Gestaltist asks again, "What are you aware of now?" This may be continued for some time. The use of this approach often leads to unexpected and highly meaningful discoveries. While awareness may begin by such superficial things as being cognizant of sitting in a chair or the fact that the nose itches, it often leads to a deeper awareness. Pain in one's heart or a burning sensation in the foot may, when worked on, lead to an awareness of some previously unrecognized unfinished business. Had such a session proceeded only on an intellectual level, such unfinished business probably would not have been discovered.

It is because of an emphasis on the body and the use of the awareness continuum that the Gestalt approach is often referred to as a body therapy. In a sense, it is a body therapy, but it is more than that since it also emphasizes interpersonal communication and the more global relationship of the human organism to the environment which sustains it.

Another characteristic of the Gestalt approach is that it tends to question questions. The Gestaltist rather routinely seeks to discern the real question from the pseudoquestion. Questions too often block communication rather than foster it and hinder discovery rather than promote it. After a speaker has presented material to a group, an audience member commonly gets up and asks a question. However, before long we note that the question has really turned into a speech in which the questioner is expounding his or her point of view on a particular subject. The Gestaltist will often ask a questioner to turn the question into a statement to test its true nature. For example, if a group member asks, "Why does Joe always defend himself when someone gives him negative feedback?" the facilitator might encourage that person to try to turn the question into a statement. The result might be that the group member would say, "I perceive Joe as defending himself whenever he gets negative feedback." By making such a statement the group member takes responsibility for his own perceptions, as well as fostering more direct communication.

GAMES

The way in which the above *rules* are utilized in a Gestalt group, or in individual sessions, is through the use of *games*. (Remember that these words are used somewhat "tongue in cheek.") The following are some of the ways that Gestaltists work with people according to the Gestalt rules. It will be remembered that all or one of these may be used, and that creativity on the part of the Gestaltist is the rule rather than the exception. If this is not the case, then we have only the use of gimmicks and not true Gestalt work.

Games of Dialogue

In this technique the Gestaltist helps a person attempt to integrate split-off aspects of their personal experience. The focus here is not dialoguing with other persons, but dialogue with the self. If, for example, a person reports difficulty in expressing warm feelings toward others, it might be suggested that a dialogue be established with the warm feelings or with the impediments to the expression of those feelings. A man might be asked, for example, to carry on a dialogue with the feminine side of his personality, and a woman might be asked to carry on a dialogue with the masculine aspects of her personality.

Making the Rounds

When the Gestaltist sees a person failing to take responsibility by generalizing, for example, it may be suggested that they "make the rounds." It would work this way. Let us presume that a person in the group makes a statement like, "I get angry at people a lot and control my anger more than is good for me." It could be suggested that this person get up and go around the group, standing in front of each person and saying, "The way I control my anger is . . . " and then finish that statement with each person. This has been found to be a very powerful way of helping a person get in touch with the *how* of control, while at the same time fostering direct "I"and "Thou" communication.

Unfinished Business

Whenever unfinished business is identified, the Gestaltist works with the person to promote closure. We often find feelings that have not been given expression. One of the most common is in relation to grief. Here the Gestaltist helps the individual work toward expression in whatever way seems most appropriate. It might be suggested, for example, that the individual recall the lost person in fantasy and carry on a conversation with that person.

In one large group session of nearly a hundred people a Gestaltist had the group break up into dyads, with each person telling the other what things were still unfinished for them. What kind of things were shared and worked on in this session? Failing to say good-bye to a parent who has died; the loss of a spouse that we had never talked about; the loss of a pet over which we had never allowed ourselves to cry; moving from the old family home without ever expressing any emotion; and anger at a boss that we never dared to express. When we became aware of such things the next step was to begin talking about them as openly as possible, expressing feelings. Letting tears flow, letting laughter flow, being spontaneous. The result of this experiment in finishing unfinished business proved to be extremely effective. This is but one example of how we might finish unfinished business. Other ways of doing this are often discovered in the immediate context of a given Gestalt session.

I Take Responsibility

In this game the individual is asked to add that phrase after reporting a particular awareness. This may come at any point in a Gestalt session, but it is quite often used at the beginning of a session. The group may begin by having each group member make a statement reporting a present awareness. A person might say, for example, "I am aware that the chair I am sitting on is hard." It would then be suggested that the phrase be added, "and I take responsibility for that." Another person might say, "I am aware that I have a headache." It would be suggested that the phrase be added, "and I take responsibility for that." If the person responds by saying, "I am aware that I have a headache—and I *don't* take responsibility for that!" we can be quite sure that there is some lack of integration here. This may call for some type of Gestalt work, presuming that the person is willing to work on it, of course.

We all tend to find it easier to claim positive awareness than negative awareness, and oftentimes we have to work very hard to claim responsibility for things like our anger or confusion.

I Have a Secret

Here the Gestaltist may suggest that each person think of something that has never been shared with anyone, a well-guarded secret. The person is not asked to share the secret, but simply bring it to mind. "How do you feel about this?" It is the feeling that is shared with the group. Feelings of shame and guilt often surface and can then be worked on in appropriate ways.

Another version of this game was demonstrated when a Gestaltist gave each person an index card and asked them to list three things they would like others to know about them on one side of the card, and three things they would not want others to know about them on the other side of the card. In the group context the three things that each wanted others to know was shared. This led to considerable new awareness when it was realized that there were often things which others shared, often even boasted about, that others felt guilty about and did not want to share.

Playing the Projection

Projections are commonly used in escaping responsibility and this game helps a person become aware that projection is taking place. For example, if a member of a Gestalt group were to say to other members of the group, "I can't trust you, I can't trust any of you," that person might be asked to say to each member of the group, "The way I don't trust you is . . . " and then finish the statement. It is often noted that if trust is really not an issue, the person may be able to do this with little difficulty, reporting that it just doesn't seem to fit. However, if trust is an issue, the person may either refuse to do the suggested activity or may report, after having done it, that it does seem to fit.

Reversals

This game is often helpful in assisting an individual to get in touch with hidden potential by exploring that individuals methods of blocking its expression. It might be suggested, for example, that a very shy person take an aggressive stance toward the group. I observed one occasion in which an individual became so in touch with latent aggressiveness that he was truly shocked, and then delighted, to find that he actually had no difficulty at all doing what he had always wanted to do—when someone else gave him permission. The next step was, of course, to give himself permission.

The Rhythm of Contact and Withdrawal

Gestalt work allows for the ebb-and-flow of attention and awareness. The natural process of life is characterized by contact and withdrawal. One gestalt is completed and recedes, then another comes to the fore. The Gestaltist may call attention to such withdrawal to see whether it is restorative or whether it is an escape from encounter with self or others. The Gestaltist might ask such questions as, where do you go when you withdraw? Can you share it with us? Can you claim it for yourself? At times a focus in this area leads to needed Gestalt work, while at other times it does not. Here again, the Gestaltist works like an artist, helping to give expression to the unique gestalt that has formed in the present situation.

Rehearsal

Occasionally, a person might be asked to share their thinking with the group. For example, someone says, "I have been thinking a lot about that." This person may be asked to share this thinking. It was Fritz's observation that most of what is referred to as "thinking" is, in reality, a rehearsing of role behavior. The individual fantasizes about what might be done or said. Then the person visualizes what will happen in response to that, etc. In fact, a great deal of so-called anxiety may often be the result of inner rehearsing. By bringing this process to awareness, the individual is often able to better understand the dynamics of their own inner processes. Through examining our processes we are able to see many of the ways that we program ourselves and hence cut ourselves off from authentic encounters.

Exaggeration

Quite often the Gestaltist may suggest that a certain body movement or a certain tone of voice be exaggerated. For example, a person may exhibit a slight wave of the hand as he talks. It may be suggested that this movement be increased, exaggerated; to take it to its rightful limit, or even beyond. *What* is it saying? *How* is it saying it? Can you enter into dialogue with it? What does dialogue say to you? Oftentimes this technique is used in relation to verbal production, as well as to other games. Let us suppose that, while working on some unfinished business through dialogue, a person says in a voice that is hardly more than a whisper, "I hate you." It might be suggested that this be repeated again, only more loudly. This same phrase might be repeated again and again, until the person literally screams, "I hate you!" Such exaggeration often has a cathartic effect that leads to new awareness.

May I Feed You a Sentence?

At times the Gestalt facilitator may see an attempt at expression on the part of a group member that the person cannot articulate; or perhaps a person's behavior is betraying a feeling or attitude of which the person is not aware. The facilitator might say, "May I feed you a sentence . . . try this on . . . say this to the group . . . ," then suggests the sentence.

This is not intended to be interpretation, but simply a way of promoting awareness. Suppose that a person has been telling the group consistently how they like everybody in the group, denying any negative feelings. Yet, it has been observed that the person has repeatedly exhibited clenched fists, or there is an angry tone in the voice. The facilitator might suggest, "Say to the group, 'In my head I like you, but inside I'm really angry at you'." Again, how this person responds will usually signal whether it is accurate. Usually, denial of the request indicates that the person is not ready to take responsibility.

OTHER RESOURCES

As was indicated previously, Gestalt work is infinitely variable and adaptable. In addition to the games that have already been discussed, there are several other techniques that have been used in Gestalt work.

Fantasy Journeys

One technique that is often used to help people develop an awareness of preconscious material is called the fantasy journey. The Gestaltist usually asks the individual(s) to close their eyes, relax, and follow the instructions that are given. The person(s) may be led on a journey to the campfire of "the wise old man" or "the wise old woman," and it is suggested that one question be asked. The results of such a fantasy are usually shared with the entire group. This has been found to be a very powerful tool and often leads to catharsis. It may also yield awareness of such things as unfinished business or hidden potential. The therapeutic possibilities of such journeys seem almost endless.

Dream Integration

A great deal of emphasis has been placed on working with dreams. It will be noted that we speak of dream *integration* rather than interpretation. The Gestaltist asks that a person retell the dream as though it is occurring in the present. When this has been done it is suggested that the person act out or "be" each part of the dream. Such activity helps the individual assimilate many of the split-off aspects of personality. Perls suggested that if a person could thoroughly integrate all of the parts of even one dream, full integration could be achieved. In a later chapter we will give extended consideration to examples of pastors in a dream seminar.

The Hot Seat

Perhaps one of the best-known resources used by Perls was what he called the hot seat. He would have an empty chair beside him and invite anyone who wanted to work to come and sit on that seat. Another empty chair would generally be nearby. This proved to be very effective, especially in helping people focus on personal issues. When this technique is used most of the interaction is limited to the facilitator and the person on the hot seat, although others might be involved from time to time. Operating within Gestalt rules, Perls might use any of the games or techniques that we have discussed, or create new ones on the spot. Quite often the person would be asked to put a person, or whatever might be needing work, in the other chair which was present and carry on a dialogue, changing chairs at times and continuing the dialogue.

It is often observed that while using the hot seat in a group, other group members who are not "working" are still very much involved in what is taking place. Others often share the same issue being dealt with by the person "working" in the hot seat. Group sharing at the end of a person's work often reveals this clearly.

Pillow Talk

Still another technique by one Gestaltist has been called pillow talk. In this approach a pillow is placed in the center of the floor, and the person who is working is asked to sit on one side of the pillow. The person is then invited to explore some dichotomy: "What is the *yes* sitting on this side of the pillow? What is the *no* on the other side of the pillow?" This may lead to considerable dialogue and movement from one side of the pillow to the other. When this dialogue has reached an impasse, or when there has been some integration, the person is asked to move to the third side of the pillow. From this vantage point it is suggested that the dialogue between the other two sides of the pillow can be seen in an objective way. Where does this side need to give in a little; what does the other side not see? etc. Then it is suggested that the person move to the fourth side of the pillow and transcend the situation. The final step consists of literally jumping onto the middle of the pillow. Johnson, who originated this way of working, has found it to be a very effective approach in helping people claim more of their larger self.[5]

Gestalt Experiments

Sometimes people inquire if it is necessary to be in a formal individual or group setting to do Gestalt work. The answer is no. In fact, Fritz and his colleagues worked out a series of experiments which could be used in a variety of settings. They provided ways of gaining awareness and moving toward personal integration and authenticity. These are published in *Gestalt Therapy*.[6] They grouped these experiments in two broad categories. The first category, called "orienting the self," utilized three types of experiments.

1. *Contacting the environment.* The types of experiments that fall under this category were feeling the actual, sensing opposed forces, attending and concentrating, and differentiating and unifying.
2. *Techniques of awareness.* These consisted of activities related to remembering, sharpening the body sense, experiencing the continuity of emotion, verbalizing, and integrating awareness.
3. *Directed awareness.* These dealt with converting confluence into contact and changing anxiety into excitement.

The second category of their experiments dealt with manipulating the self:

1. *Retroflection.* The experimenter investigates misdirected behavior, mobilizing the muscles, and executing the re-reversed act.
2. *Introjection.* This concerns introjects and eating, and dislodging and digesting introjects.
3. *Projections.* These lead toward discovering projections and assimilating them.

These experiments can, of course, be done in a group setting as well as by an individual although some of them require more than one person in their performance.

Again, we may emphasize that the variety of such techniques seems almost endless. However, it needs to be remembered that none of these techniques should be used as gimmicks or in an indiscriminate way, but should always take into account the needs of those persons with whom they are used. When used appropriately and sensitively, they can be vehicles of profound personal growth.

Why are such activities found to be so effective? It is because, as Zimmer notes, knowledge and action are inseparable. It is through the actual experience of a particular role or action that we are realize the truth that is inherent there.[7]

A PERSPECTIVE ON PSYCHODYNAMICS

To really know what an onion is, we need to always bring back our focus of attention to the onion as a whole, rather than focusing exclusively on its parts. What the onion has, which the parts do not, is the quality of wholeness. At the same time, had we never seen an onion before, it might be helpful for us to focus our attention alternately on the various parts. We could observe size and shape, the way it consists of layers, its characteristic smell, the way it feels, etc. Each awareness brings us to a new Gestalt in relation to the onion, with such Gestalts dissolving (becoming ground) and forming (becoming figure) as our attention moves from one aspect to another. Then, at some point it all fits together, and we exclaim, "Aha, this is an onion."

In a sense, the "rules and games" of Gestalt are like the layers of an onion. They are parts of a total Gestalt and must not be confused with that totality. The Gestalt approach is the ground against which the various figures emerge. Each consideration of the figures (i.e., rules, techniques, and games) further enriches our understanding of the whole.

Another figure that enriches the whole is the Gestalt perspective on psychodynamics. Whereas Freud formulated much of his theory around the outline of id, ego, and superego, Perls' unique view centered around three zones of experience: the exterior, middle, and interior zones of experience. Figure 3.1 will help to visualize these zones.

1. *The exterior zone.* Exterior experience comes through the senses as they contact the immediate environment.
2. *The interior zone.* Interior experience takes place within the organism, such as hunger, thirst, and including all actions of the organism that accomplish the maintenance of homeostasis, some of which we are aware of, and some of which we are not.
3. *The middle zone.* This zone, which Perls often referred to as the DMZ (the demilitarized zone), is the point of contact between internal and external experience. The controlling function of this zone is thought. It is in this zone that we find the memories, the labels, the wishes—things which are processed by the mind through *thinking*. Perls preferred to call this activity *fantasy*. The reason for this was to clearly distinguish it from either the internal or external reality. From the Gestalt perspective, much of what is called neurotic behavior originates in the DMZ. It occurs when the activity in this area is confused with reality.

This is the reason for the principle of the *now,* which we considered at the beginning of this chapter—to help the person sort out the fantasy of the DMZ from the reality of internal and external experience. The games of the Gestalt approach provide situations in which the person is confronted with experience in its immediacy, without the distortions of the DMZ. Only when distortions of this zone are set aside can the organism function in a healthy way. This may be seen as a parallel conception to that proposed by Albert Ellis in his Rational-Emotive Therapy (RET).[8] A given event is responded to according to the belief system that a person holds. Therefore, if we hold irrational beliefs, we may react to an event in an entirely inappropriate way. The difference between Gestalt and Rational-Emotive Therapy is found primarily in the way in which therapeutic intervention takes place. Ellis would correct the irrational thinking through the use of more thinking, while Perls would seek to do it through experiential activities.

FIGURE 3.1. The Gestalt Onion

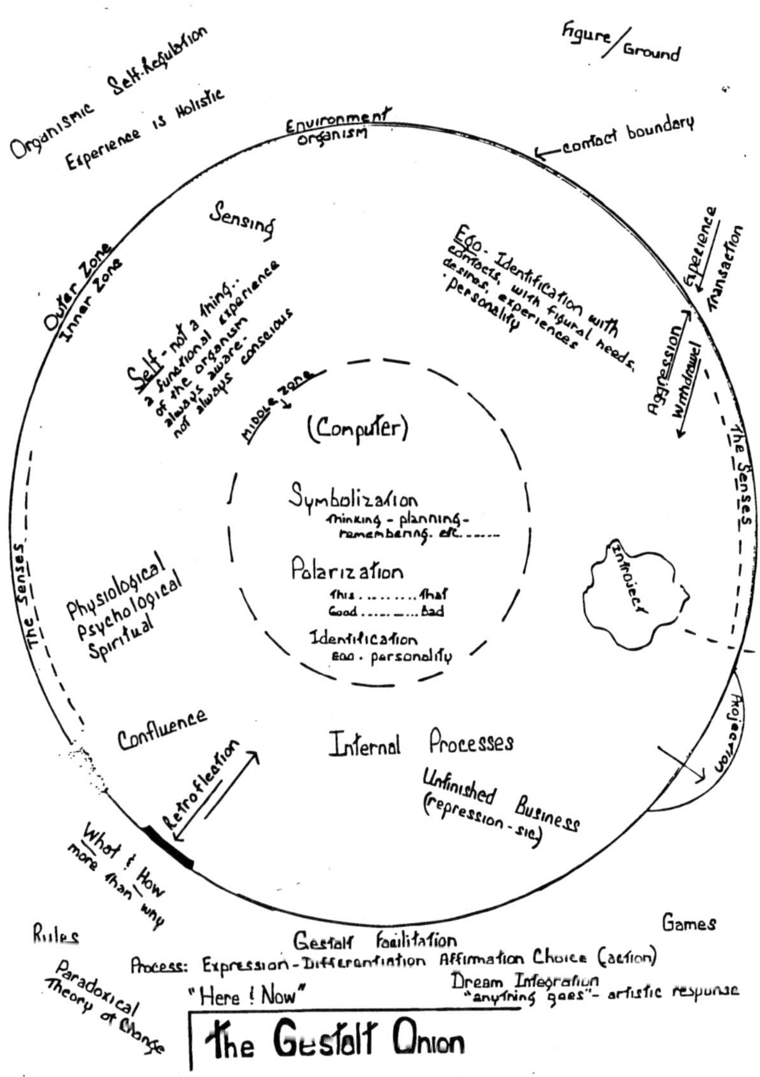

Fritz saw the DMZ as containing, for most people, too many shoulds and oughts, introjections, and value judgments, which keep external and internal experience from standing on their own. Instead, the "computer" programs (thinking) of the DMZ contaminate experience. Gestalt insists that experience has its own validity, and that we must be open to the wisdom of the entire organism and not be controlled by the thinking process.

Let me give an illustration involving one of the seminarians in a clinical pastoral education (CPE) program. This seminarian, a very gifted and intelligent woman, received some rather negative feedback from a patient about the work she was doing in pastoral care. As a result of this feedback, she began to see negative criticism all around her, and she also became very self-critical. She *should* have done better, she said. She was sure that I must have a low evaluation of her because of what had happened. She was also quite convinced that other staff members must feel the same, and she began to interpret certain things that had been said and done in a way that confirmed this conclusion. She became quite upset and was not quite sure she could return to the hospital floor to which she was assigned for her clinical experience in pastoral care.

When she came to me for help I suggested to her that she check out the reality of how she was actually being seen, experientially. In a manner quite similar to what might be done in a Gestalt group session I suggested that she, (1) fully claim how she was presently feeling, and (2) ask others directly how they felt about her work.

She started by sharing with the group with whom she was involved in the training program. She shared with them the negative incident with the patient including the feelings and attitudes she had experienced in relation to the incident. To her surprise, she found the group very accepting of where she was and what she was experiencing. They said to her, in effect, "Yes, it looks like you could have done better with this patient, but it's all right with us if you're not perfect."

She also established direct communication with several of the staff members in regard to how we viewed her work. She was told that we liked what she was doing and, furthermore, this was the only incident of negative feedback concerning her up to this point in the program. When she asked me what I thought about the incident in question, I said, "I think you have an opportunity here to learn something about yourself, if you choose to. I never expected you to be perfect. Is that what you expect of yourself?" She replied spontaneously, "Well, since everyone else seems OK about who I am, I guess it's all right for me to be me, without being perfect." She then went back to the hospital floor with more confidence in herself and her pastoral work, knowing that she was doing the best she could do, and that there was no need for her to be so hard on herself.

Applying our perspective of the zones of experience, we would say that her external experience was distorted by the activity of the middle zone, where she applied should and oughts to the experience. She reacted on the basis of her "experience about experience," rather than letting the experience simply be what it was. The activity of the middle zone distorted her perception of the experience, resulting in negative self-evaluation and distorting contacts with other persons and her environment.

Although this student moved quickly beyond the distortions of the middle zone, this is not always the case, especially when the middle zone is heavily laden with identification with past experience, or when there is a large content of introjects. While Freud used the concept of repression to explain the hold of past experience on present feeling and behavior, Fritz preferred to talk of unfinished business, believing that the usual formulation of repression was too static a concept.

From the Gestalt perspective, the human organism contains a natural and powerful need for wholeness and completeness. As the organism moves toward wholeness and completeness, experiences from the past that have not been resolved continue to seek resolution. They surface individually in relation to the predominant need of the organism. They limit present functioning to a greater or lesser degree, depending on their quality of importance to the individual, as well as their sheer quantity. The perspective that Gestalt brings is that of allowing for the completion of incomplete gestalten in a dynamic way in the present, rather than by attempting the impossible—going back into the past. Completing unfinished business in a present-centered frame of reference is the primary purpose of the games of Gestalt.

Another important aspect of the Gestalt perspective has to do with its view of ego and self. Identification with our experience is seen as a function which is called *ego*. In other words, ego is not seen as a thing in itself but a function of the organism. The ego is the mobilizing function through which the organism taps its energy and resources for meeting needs. In Fritz's words, "The ego in a kind of administrative function will connect the actions of the whole organism with its foremost needs . . ."[9]

In the Gestalt approach, the self has a different meaning than ego. Fritz said, "The self is the contact-boundary at work; its activity is forming figures and grounds."[10] Perhaps an illustration will help make the meaning of self clearer. I sit here writing this book. I am deeply concentrating on what I am writing. It is as though there is nothing in the world but me, my manuscript, and my computer. Then suddenly, I spring from my chair without thinking and dash into the next room. My daughter has screamed and I make an instantaneous response. This is the self at work. The self is always at the contact-boundaries, and we may or may not be conscious of it at work. Fritz said of the self, "It is the artist of life. It is only a small factor in the total organism/environment interaction, but it plays the crucial role of finding and making the roles we grow by."[11]

Following through on the illustration above, we may say that it is through ego-function that I am writing this book. My ego organizes my actions and my thoughts in such a way that I am able to produce the words which you now read. In reality, this is a very complicated task. It requires being in tune with both inner and outer zones of experience and careful processing in the inner zone. My ego also provides motivation for my task: It assigns a positive value to what I do and I am pleased and feel fulfilled when I step back and look at my work. Yet also a part of me is separate from all of that, as was displayed when my daughter screamed, overriding the immediate concern of the ego. This is my self, and I also realize that it is *I* who steps back from the immediate involvement. I am still somehow more than all that. I am my self.

From the Gestalt perspective, psychological health is seen as coming from identification with the self, and disease is the result of alienation from the self. Identification with the self naturally carries creative excitement. Identification with ego results in loss of spontaneity and excitement. The games, techniques, and resources that we considered in this chapter all have one primary goal—"to train the ego, the various identifications and alienations, by experiments and deliberate awareness of one's various functions, until the sense is spontaneously revived that 'it is I who am thinking, perceiving, feeling, and doing this.' At this point the patient can take over on his own."[12]

When this point has been reached, it may be said that we have a state of organismic self-regulation. Life is characterized by the spontaneous completion of each emerging gestalt. Theoretically, ego is no longer needed at this point because it has been transcended. This is the transpersonal experience of which we spoke in the first chapter of this book. The transpersonal experience has been central to the Christian understanding of spiritual growth and is the type of spiritual experience that is within the potential of each person. It is a sense of the unity of God that excludes the function of ego and unites the person with the true self.

Yet, if we are to live in the world, we cannot always exist in this mountain-top experience. We still need our feet on the ground. We still need healthy ego functioning to define existential boundaries and to allow for necessary contact with our environment. So the question is not if we need to retain ego-functioning but how to do so in a healthy way. It means that the ego must become the servant of the self, rather than the self becoming subservient to the ego. When the ego is in control its main characteristic is an unhealthy pride that is, in the final analysis, destructive.

Chapter 4

Once Upon a Time

I am feeling somewhat exhausted from writing the first three chapters. They seem to contain too much head-stuff. I wonder if I have really communicated anything about the Gestalt approach or if my efforts have resulted in obfuscation?

As I recall Perls' statement that any theory should be capable of being stated in simple terms, I am reminded of when my three-year-old daughter brought a book home from the library that contained an old Austrian folktale called *The Magic Wall.*[1] It occurs to me that the story is a paradigm of our present life experience. It seems a perfect background against which to make a simple statement about the Gestalt approach. Although the story begins with the well-known words "Once upon a time" and purports to tell about the past, it invites us to experience the story in our here-and-now awareness.

Once upon a time King Frederick lived in a castle with his family. His castle was cheerful and gay. It was different from other castles in that it had no wall around it, no moat. The King and his family (and ducks and cats and dogs) mixed freely with the villagers, and life was good and fulfilling. Even the Queen felt free to argue with the village merchants about the high price of fresh vegetables.

In other words, life is flowing along in a natural rhythm. We can identify with this. It is the way we fantasize life as being and continuing on forever.

Then one day a neighboring king, by the name of Bertram, came to the village with his armor clanging and with foot soldiers in accompaniment. Bertram insisted that Frederick was living a most unkingly life and said he would show Frederick how a king really ought to live. Although Frederick was contented with his life, he went along with the suggestion because he didn't want to offend his neighbor.

We certainly can identify with that. Who among us has not, at one time or another, done things because we did not want to offend someone else, even though we would rather not have done it? I certainly have.

Bertram had a well-fortified castle with soldiers to guard it. No one could get in without the king's permission, and the villagers were intimidated by the king. A deep moat surrounded the castle, which added to its isolation, and life was very much controlled. Bertram insisted that Frederick's castle should be the same. So they went back to Frederick's castle, and following Bertram's advice, Frederick forced the villagers to build a wall around the castle. Then the villagers were forced to build a moat around the walls. Armed soldiers were put on the walls. When Frederick appeared to be safe and secure in his castle, Bertram returned to his own castle, congratulating himself on his good deed.

So it sounds as if things are really getting better, particularly now that Bertram is going to live like a real king.

But as it turned out, life really was not all secure and comfortable for Frederick and his family. For one thing, the villagers grew suspicious about what was going on behind those high walls surrounding the castle. The royal children sat glumly in the dark castle garden. The soldiers guarding the castle fought amongst themselves. Even the dogs and cats seemed to be unhappy, and the Queen did not go into the village to argue with the merchants about the price of food any more. King Frederick grew depressed and wondered how he let this all happen. He found that the walls kept enemies out but they also kept out friends. Even the royal cats and dogs tried to jump the wall to join their friends. The formerly happy castle became a place of misery. In modern terms we would say that the place was characterized by neurotic living.

King Frederick paced, wondered, thought. How could he get out of the mess he was in? How did it all happen anyway? He had not asked for this to happen. Why did it all happen? But all of his pacing, all of his thinking, all of his attempts to answer the question *why* accomplished absolutely nothing. He felt stuck.

This story certainly would be a "downer" if it stopped here. But we are told that King Frederick finally went to work on his own situation, literally. He took his pickaxe and started to tear down the wall. Soon others began to help him. Before long the walls and towers were down, the moat was filled with the debris, and the castle looked as it had before. Now the Queen again complained about the high cost of vegetables in the village, the royal dogs and cats frolicked with their friends in the village, and there was joy and happiness all around.

But wait—the villain returns! King Bertram decided that if his neighbor was so foolish as to leave himself defenseless, he is practically asking to have his castle taken away from him. So Bertram came with his armor clanging and with his soldiers, and was about to take the castle!

King Frederick however, said that this will not happen because he has a "magic wall." As Bertram started to attack he suddenly understood what this meant. The villagers formed a living wall around Frederick's castle, and the goatherds appeared on the mountain peaks ready to roll stones down on Bertram's soldiers. Naturally, Bertram decided to retreat, puzzled and envious.

Life returned to normal, and the pulsating activity of the castle and village continued in natural and spontaneous cycles. Life became fully human. People (and dogs and cats and geese and ducks) met at their center of vital awareness.

GESTALTING THE FOLKTALE

At this point, we will seek to lift up the lively figure of the Gestalt approach against the ground of the folktale. One of the things that immediately stands out about this tale is how easily we can resonate with the naturalness and spontaneity of the king's life. We might well say that everything here is in a state of organismic self-regulation.

But as the tale unfolds we see that the natural ebb-and-flow of life takes a sudden turn for the worse, and neurotic living prevails. Certainly, nobody wanted this to happen. But happen it does, and this is true to life experience. We intend to lead natural, satisfying lives that are without conflict, but somehow things just do not always work out that way. Before we know it, we find that our lives seem to be filled with chaos. When this happens we usually blame the chaos on someone else and not ourselves. What is it that makes life turn out this way?

In King Frederick's case we can identify the results of an unhealthy confluence. He is so naive. He wants to please everyone. He thinks everybody else must want what is best for him. King Frederick has no boundaries. He cannot separate his desires from others' desires. He cannot say "no." He is in an unhealthy state of confluence, and he has a hard struggle ahead of him before he can overcome this block to healthy functioning. The walls start going up and the natural rhythm of life is broken.

We also see here a very unhealthy introjection. Frederick took in someone else's idea of what it meant to be a king and acted on that—with disastrous results! Bertram's ideas obviously do not fit Frederick's life. Yet, Frederick took in the idea whole and swallowed it indiscriminately. It was like eating a sandwich in a plastic bag.

We may also surmise that there is more than a little projection in King Frederick's situation. Just as Adam projected responsibility onto Eve, and Eve projected it onto the serpent, so King Frederick projects responsibility onto King Bertram. Bertram is the cause of all his trouble. Bertram made him do it, he thinks.

As King Frederick sits in his throne room thinking about his situation we can see him getting very depressed. He sits on the anger that should appropriately go out toward Bertram and thereby retroflects it, probably experiencing a great deal of self-pity as his depression deepens.

King Frederick is a figure with whom we can identify rather easily. After King Bertram's visit he feels trapped in a life run by rules that are not of his own liking. His life is drained of joy, and he is literally heartsick. He may well have consulted his physicians about heart palpitations and may have been manifesting symptoms of high blood pressure.

King Frederick, in his plight, represents many of us who are caught in roles, experiencing their artificiality, but not knowing what to do about it. Frederick wants to do something about it, and yet he does not. He may even be embarrassed by who he is, make halfhearted attempts to be himself, but quickly lose courage and revert back to being what he feels he is not. He keeps asking himself *why* all this has happened, and he chases the answers in a never ending, widening circle. He certainly is a very ineffective king at this point.

Little wonder that his subjects are bewildered and confused. "They stared at the bleak castle walls and high towers. They muttered among themselves, 'what is the king up to?' "[2]

At this point it seems that the walls are not only around the castle, but also very tightly around King Frederick. He is "walled up" in his throne room. We suspect he is in a state of high anxiety. He walks back and forth, but he does not go anywhere. The Gestaltist would identify this as the impasse. One of the characteristics of this state is *implosion*. Implosion means that the energy is turned inward, toward oneself, the result being such symptoms as depression. *Phobic behavior* is also another characteristic of this state. In a paradoxical way, we find ourselves not doing what we know we need to do. We may safely assume that King Frederick has an idea of what type of action is needed but simply ran ideas around in his head (ran his computer), instead of taking that action.

This is a dangerous point in life experience. It is a point at which there is little authentic life, where the center of vital awareness is not being touched. Suicide may be seriously considered. Attempts at self-expression may be inappropriate. A person who is at this point may rationalize criminal behavior, or life may display neurotic behavior.

Much of traditional counseling has been of little help to people at an impasse because it has provided them with reasons for their behavior without actually helping them take responsibility and change their behavior. It is easier to talk about reasons for behavior than it is to change behavior. We tend to take the easy way out. It is also easier to talk about what one proposes to do tomorrow than to take action and be responsible for the present moment.

How does King Frederick escape the neurotic life experience in which he finds himself? Very simply. "He stomped outside carrying his pickaxe."[3] He simply let himself do what he knew needed to be done. He let the unfinished gestalt complete itself.

It is not surprising that life again takes on its full ebb-and-flow in both castle and village. The wall is torn down, King Frederick has face-to-face confrontation with King Bertram, and he shows he has the power to be who he is—and that is all it takes. When the old problem starts to return, we see the real payoff. Frederick is not defenseless now. He can take care of what life sends his way and can interact effectively with life. He now has a magic wall. He possesses new strength and spontaneity. He has become fully human. His life is truly good and can now take on its dynamic ebb-and-flow. He is in touch with his spirit, his soul.

King Frederick's movement to personal authenticity is a natural process, as it is for all of us. All that anyone can do is to help facilitate that process. Because we have a tendency to seriously block the natural process, this help is oftentimes greatly needed. How might a Gestaltist facilitate the process? From what perspective does the facilitator come? Are there identifiable techniques that a Gestaltist might use? What are the resources that the Gestaltist brings?

MEANWHILE, BACK AT THE CASTLE

To answer these questions let's return to King Frederick, who is locked up in his castle. We find him in his throne room in a state of agitated depression.

He has tried to change his situation by manipulating his own ideas. He has said things to himself like, "I don't want to offend King Bertram." "Maybe it is really all my fault. I should have had more courage." "I ought to be a better king than this." "I'll just never be able to measure up to all this." "It would make good sense just to jump from the tower."

Frederick is a very miserable person, indeed. He has gone from being a beloved king who moved freely among the people, to being an isolated man shut up with his own thoughts and fantasies, more dead than alive. He has arrived at the impasse.

Now let us suppose that a Gestaltist has access to the throne room, say in the guise of a priest or a jester. What could be done to help the king? What might facilitate King Frederick's movement toward resolving the impasse? Having considered Gestalt games and resources in the previous chapter, let's see how we might utilize some of them to help King Frederick.

First and foremost, the Gestaltist would not have worked to help the king figure out *why* he was in the fix he was in. Instead, there would be an emphasis on the *what* and *how.*

It would have been a ticklish situation for the jester or the priest, but the following might have been said: "What are you feeling right now, O King? A tightness in your head? How do you do that to yourself? Who would you like to squeeze in the way that you are squeezing your own head? Was Bertram really responsible for that wall being built? Can you take responsibility for that? Say, '*I* let the wall be built around the castle, *I* take responsibility for that.' Say it again and again, louder and louder! Can you hear yourself saying it?"

"Put King Bertram over in that other chair. What would you really like to say to him? What would you really like to do to him? Go ahead and do it. That's right, hit him again, harder and harder. Now what do you really want?"

We can be quite sure that helping King Frederick move toward more spontaneous behavior and regaining the natural ebb-and-flow of his life would not be an easy task. While theoretically he might be able to do this at any moment, we suspect that his heavy involvement in the king role, and the rather extreme state of his agitated depression, will require quite a bit of Gestalt work. It isn't hard to say, "I take responsibility for the wall being built," but does he? What other unfinished business does he have? Who told him that kings must always go along with what another king tells them to do? Put that person in a chair. Create a dialogue. Or he may be encouraged to explore his fantasies about the kind of king he would really like to be, and what he would really like to do. Or perhaps he could work on dream integration, exploring the meaning of the puzzling dreams he has been having.

We can imagine that there are times when King Frederick is about to give up. But if he is willing to keep at it and refrains from beheading the Gestaltist's, we would expect that slowly and painfully King Frederick will begin to gain an awareness of who he is and what he wants. As he does this, we would say that he undoes an unhealthy confluence. As he gradually lets go of the ideas of what a king should be, he is undoing the introjection that keeps him from being authentic. As he confronts ideas like, "King Bertram made me build this wall," he is in a position to claim his projections and take responsibility for his actions. As he becomes more aware of how he is turning his anger upon himself, rather than letting it go out toward Bertram, he begins to undo the retroflection that has nearly destroyed him.

Thus, the confluence becomes contact, introjection gives way to individuality, projection gives way to being responsible, and retroflecting activity is reversed so that energy flows outward in spontaneous and appropriate activity.

King Frederick has now reached what Gestaltists would call the stage of *explosion,* and that is exactly what happened in the tale. "He stomped outside carrying his pickaxe."[4] He literally came alive again. He is in touch with his spirit, his life. His enthusiasm is contagious.

The tragic scene is a tragic scene no more! He is now engaging life at the center of his vital awareness.

In the Gestalt approach all of our movement is seen as being toward spontaneity and authentic expressiveness. It is only when this occurs that there is any real closure in a given situation. King Frederick moves from the inner turmoil, the isolation of his own fantasies and thinking, and his own alienation from himself and others to spontaneous expressiveness that brings about a happy ending.

Personal growth is usually not easy and involves a very real struggle. It is to gain a glimpse of this struggle in the "physician of the soul" that we turn to in the next chapter as we as pastors take a taste of our own medicine.

Chapter 5

A Taste of Our Own Medicine

In the previous chapter I sought to provide a broad "feeling" for the Gestalt approach through the Austrian folktale. Now I want to narrow the focus somewhat. Since this book is about pastoral care and counseling, I want to bring the pastor more clearly into focus. If the pastor intends to use a Gestalt perspective, he or she must have personal experience in this approach. We must take a taste of our own medicine before we can prescribe it to others.

AWARENESS

As I have already indicated, Gestalt is characterized by innovation and creativity, and it carries with it a sense of excitement. In learning to do pastoral care and counseling, it is necessary that we feel some of the excitement of discovery about ourselves. It is this very excitement that is the indicator of growth.

Right before his death, in 1969, Perls wrote in an author's note to a new edition of *Gestalt Therapy*, "I now consider that neurosis is not a sickness but one of several symptoms of growth stagnation."[1] From his point of view, our lack of growth, our unwillingness to grow, is at the core of those intense personal difficulties that have often been referred to as disease. When growth does not proceed normally, human lives are distorted into an endless variety of self-defeating and fractured patterns.

Growth naturally occurs when there is free-flowing organismic/environment interaction. The Gestalt approach is seen as nothing more than the "original, undistorted, natural approach to life; that is, to man's thinking, acting, feeling."[2] The organism naturally assimilates what is needed from the environment for growth. This is done through a natural process of gestalt formation that consists of contact, sensing, and excitement. Awareness is at the center of the process and, in one sense, it *is* the process. For this reason, Gestalt has focused on the conscious rather than the unconscious, on the known rather than the unknown, the here and now rather than the there and then.

With what are we in contact? What senses do we use in achieving awareness? How is our awareness determined? How do we experience our excitement? When the life process is allowed to flow naturally, we have healthy living and growth. Stagnation and repression, rather than growth and development, is the result of incomplete gestalten.

Why, then, do we not all function holistically, naturally? Gestaltists say it is because we have largely cut ourselves off from our senses. The senses are the sources of our awareness. As we saw in our consideration of King Frederick, we tend to block awareness of our senses in several characteristic ways.

GESTALT EXPERIMENTS

While teaching the Gestalt approach in pastoral care and counseling, I have found it helpful to work with the experiments described in *Gestalt Therapy*.[3] The experiments are seen as ways of trying things, rather than being experiments in a strictly scientific sense. They focus on our experience and how we make contact with our environment. In what ways can we sharpen our awareness? How can we convert confluence into contact, reclaim our projections, dislodge our introjects, claim the potential of our retroflections?

Through contrived situations it is possible to learn a great deal about ourselves, what we do, and how we do it.

Feeling the Actual

One experiment I have often used with pastors is referred to as *feeling the actual*. In this experiment I give each group member a pencil and paper and ask them to write sentences beginning with "Here and now I am aware that (of) . . ." Or, "At this moment I am aware that . . ." This activity is allowed to continue until all members of the group stop writing, usually five or ten minutes. Members of the group are then asked to share what they have written, with due respect for anyone who chooses not to share. However, if a person decides not to share, that person is asked to give the reason for their decision.

The results of this initial sharing are always interesting and reveal much about the type of contact the individual has with the environment. Some pastors are only aware of the physical setting of the room. Others may describe the people in the room, but are oblivious even to the chair on which they are sitting. Still another may write only of bodily sensations.

After sharing, the group discusses the implications of this experiment for the overall pattern of our awareness. In what areas do we have awareness, and in what do we not? Some pastors seem to be unaware of their bodies and living mostly in their heads. There is, of course, no value judgment placed on reported awareness. The only purpose of such an experiment is to help the pastor realize which sources of awareness are used, and which are not. Since good contact with people presupposes the full use of sensory awareness, good contact with the environment is an important consideration.

As members of such a Gestalt group become more fully aware of themselves, they are often surprised at the many Gestalts which form and the increasing awareness which they experience at a given moment.

In the "feeling the actual" experiment, group members may be asked to think about the next thing they would have written if they had not stopped. If the pastor is willing to look seriously at this question, the very act of doing so may lead to a clearer awareness of typical patterns of avoidance.

One pastor was even uncomfortable focusing momentarily on the here and now, because when he did so he became aware of "a general uncomfortableness, a kind of pain." Another pastor stopped because he suddenly had become aware of his body, and he felt nauseated. Still another stopped because she became aware of an unresolved personal situation.

This beginning experiment usually serves as a focusing point in regard to awareness. Often a session ends with the members of the group again writing sentences beginning with "Here and now I am aware that. . . ." The difference is usually dramatic, even after such a brief exercise in awareness.

One result of developing simple sensory awareness is that it can enrich interpersonal relationships. For example, one member of a group came to a deep awareness of the table before him—its shape, texture, and uniqueness. As he became aware of the table, he found himself suddenly becoming aware of the uniqueness of the person across the table from him. Then followed a new awareness of the possibilities for an authentic relationship with that person. As we begin to see people as the unique entities that they are, it is easier for us to see ourselves more clearly as well. Consequently, it becomes easier to respect and take responsibility for ourselves. We can more readily claim our projections, and authentic relationships can develop.

An Experiment in Directed Awareness

Another interesting example of Gestalt work occurred in a group of pastors who were experimenting with introjection. This experiment sought to cultivate awareness regarding the ways in which we take things into ourselves, and how healthy assimilation can occur.

I have found that pastors tend to have considerable difficulty with introjection. All too often, pastors takes things on faith without determining whether they are appropriate or not, health giving or not. This occurs especially when such things come from religious sources to which the pastor has an allegiance. Even many things that are potentially health giving do not become so for the pastor because they are not properly processed. How might a Gestaltist help the pastor toward greater awareness? I have found an experiment in directed awareness to be helpful.

To begin this directed awareness experiment, I give an apple to each member of the group. The group members are then told to eat the apples and closely observe how they do this. After most members of the group have finished eating their apples, they are invited to share their experience with the other group members. In one session, a member of the group spent considerable time preparing his apple for eating, while another bit viciously into the apple and ate quickly. Still another chewed carefully and slowly. One person lost contact with the apple as soon as it was bitten, and another reported being conscious of the chewed and liquefied apple as it was swallowed and had a strange sensation that it became part of him. When observations were shared it was noted that there were, indeed, many differences in awareness. Several group members shared bites of each other's apples and thereby gained a new awareness of the variations in the taste of different apples.

Following this experience, the group moved naturally into a consideration of how other things in their lives were taken in. One pastor reported that he took in ideas much the same way he had eaten his apple—he had taken big bites, had not chewed thoroughly, and it hurt when it went down. Likewise, he almost literally swallowed ideas without pausing to work with them enough for proper "digestion."

One member said that he had actually not wanted to eat the apple, but he felt he had to "because it was part of the experiment." His uneasy stomach helped him to a new awareness of the dangers of taking into oneself what one does not really want.

To help this pastor deal with this tendency of taking things in rather indiscriminately, we encouraged him to act out his feelings. What was he feeling right now? He felt anger! Could he express it? He would try. He was encouraged to give himself permission to "let go." He did. The anger flowed out. He was encouraged to make a fist, something he had spontaneously started to do earlier, then stopped. He spoke of his religious superior in angry terms. When asked if he could express this anger to his superior, the pastor banged his fist on the table. Feelings flowed out, carried by harsh words that might not be expected from "a man of the cloth." When his words and actions stopped he was asked how he felt. He said he felt a sense of relief! It was good to get it out, to claim it. He had a new awareness of himself. He also later reported becoming aware of ways he had passive-aggressively blocked many of the programs and ideas of his superior, and he now felt ready to take responsibility for such actions.

As these experiments progressed, members of the group were given printed instructions relating to the experiments and were encouraged to work on the experiments at their leisure. It was rather surprising to find that one member of the group, a Baptist minister, worked on some of the experiments at home with his wife and children. These experiments can also be conducted in complete privacy, if that is what is needed.

Perhaps these brief examples will give some idea of the way in which experiments may be used to promote personal growth. By bringing our awareness to the ways we do—or do not—contact and assimilate our environment, we are in a position to move to healthier contact and behavior. We do this by using all the avenues at our disposal, namely all our senses.

Some pastors have objected to these experiments. They say that they are interested in the senses; that they are concerned with *spiritual* things. From the Gestalt standpoint this attitude betokens a misunderstanding of spirituality. As we noted in Chapter 1, the biblical perspective is that we are *one* in body and soul. We have a unitary nature. Therefore, we can not cut ourselves off from the senses of the body and still be whole persons. If we do this, we literally cut ourselves off from our own spirit. Our spirit cannot grow when we deny the reality of the sensory experience. Rather, to sharpen our contact with our environment, to claim our senses and our own spontaneous behavior, is to experience spiritual growth. To examine our behavior, to try some new types of behavior, and to be open to what we may discover about ourselves can lead to growth in an all-encompassing way. Spiritual growth is part of the process of being fully human, not something separate from it.

While these instances of the use of Gestalt experiments with pastors is by no means exhaustive, I trust that I have given some small indication of their benefit.

THE HOT SEAT

I have often worked with pastors using the hot seat. This was one of Fritz Perls' primary ways of working, his trademark. As we noted in a previous chapter, when this technique is used there is usually an empty chair beside the Gestalt facilitator, or sometimes a pillow is thrown into the middle of the group circle and an invitation is extended for someone to volunteer to work.

Facing the possibility of working on the hot seat can be very threatening. When a person contemplates doing it there is usually an internal dialogue. One side says "yes," and the other side says "no." This is a common experience and is one of the primary ways we block ourselves from healthy contact with the environment. Fritz saw this as a self-torture game and referred to it as "top dog vs. underdog." The top dog is all for perfection and is filled with shoulds and shouldn'ts, introjections that are within. Resistance and manipulations characterize the underdog. On the surface it agrees with top dog, but it sabotages the demands of the top dog. It is the underdog that usually wins. The individual is always *trying* to change, but somehow change never occurs. The underdog seems capable of rationalizing anything, and can come up with all sorts of catastrophic fantasies of what would happen if something were done or not done.

Let's look at Bob, a Roman Catholic priest who is considering hot seat work. His top dog says, "I really ought to get out there and confront my tears." The underdog replies, "But I'm not sure I'm ready. Suppose I cry. What will people think of me, a grown man, crying?" Top dog, "It's really all right if you go out there and cry." Underdog, "No, I'm too big to cry," etc.

Bob is relieved when Paul, another group member, volunteers to work on the hot seat. Now Bob can relax. He has successfully avoided getting in touch with himself. But his relaxation does not last very long because the dialogue in his head immediately resumes: Top dog, "There, look at that. Paul is beating the stuffing out of that pillow, getting in touch with his anger. He doesn't seem to mind showing some of his feelings, and he's only a seminary student!" Underdog, "I'm really a failure for not going out there. I just can't do it." Top dog, "You should be out there right now, working," etc.

After Paul has completed his work, Bob is ready to move onto the hot seat (or at least so he tells himself) when the group facilitator asks each member of the group to pick a partner they feel comfortable with. The partners are to find a corner someplace and each share with the other what they are avoiding. It is difficult, but Bob finally confides in his partner that he has a lump in his throat, which has been there for some time, and he thinks it is tears that he has been avoiding.

The hot seat is open again for someone who wants to work. This time Bob thinks he has enough courage to try it. After all, his partner did not condemn him for having a lump in his throat or for the statement that he might be holding back some tears. Bob is furiously rehearsing exactly what he will say, and how he will say, it when he notices someone else is already on the hot seat. He begins to feel a little sick inside.

Somehow, in his own way, in his own time, Bob takes responsibility and finds himself out there on the hot seat. He stopped *trying* and just did it. He wonders how he got out there. Thoughts race through his mind. What was it he was going to say? How had he rehearsed it? He finds himself shaking, his head a blur. I ask, "What are you going to work on?" Bob is now ready with his rehearsed words, his script. He decides he is going to put the lump in his throat on the pillow and talk to it. Then, he tells himself, he will change places and let it talk back to him, let it tell him what it is and what it wants from him. But no words come.

I say, "Do you notice what's happening in your body?" Bob is aware of a shaking that is engulfing his body, and that his eyes are filling with tears. He is about to speak, but before he can he finds himself collapsing on the floor, sobbing. He can't seem to stop it, and after what seems like an eternity I say, "Is there a name?" But Bob cannot find his voice, only sobs come from his mouth. Someone puts a Kleenex in his hand. After awhile I ask, "What is happening now, Bob?" Somehow words begin to come. Bob says, "My head, my damned computer." I say, "What about it?" Bob responds, "It runs all the time and I can't seem to shut it off." I gently touch him. For some reason this triggers more tears. As the tears begin to subside I say, "What's happening now?" Bob responds, "I don't know for sure. I guess my computer runs and runs and cuts me off from my feelings, (pause) and from being touched by other people, too." Bob sits there for awhile. I ask, "What do you want right now? Do you want anything from any of us?" Bob looks around at the group and seems to see people more clearly. Finally, he shyly reaches out to me and hugs me—and it feels good to me! He now resumes his place in the group circle, feeling that he is more in touch with himself. He feels he has less of a need to run his "computer" and less need to find out "the reason why."

By taking responsibility for himself, Bob has begun the difficult path toward fuller self-awareness and expressiveness. He needs a little more time to assimilate, to digest. Even his computer is silent for a time!

At the next group meeting, I once again ask the members to close their eyes, go into their bodies, and to "see" what they are aware of. They take a guided tour of their bodies. Bob makes a startling discovery—the lump in his throat is back again. It isn't quite as big now, but it certainly is there. More work to be done!

Taking the hot seat seems a little easier this time. He ignores the chatter between top dog and underdog and simply goes to the hot seat. He surprises himself by the ease with which he did it. Now that he's out there he isn't quite sure what to do; this time he does not have a script ready. I say to him, "What are you aware of right now?"

BOB: I'm aware of a lump in my throat. It's been there a long time. I guess I need to work on that.

WARD: You *guess* you need to work on that?

BOB: I mean I do want to work on it, I *do* . . . I'm so sick and tired of it being there.

WARD: Put it out there on the pillow and tell it that.

BOB: (To pillow.) I'm sick and tired of you.

WARD: What else would you like to tell it?

BOB: You choke me. You cut me off from my spontaneity. You make my priesthood difficult.

WARD: Be specific. Tell it *how* it cuts you off from your priesthood.

BOB: You cut me off from my priesthood by cutting me off from other people.

WARD: Switch—sit over there on the pillow now and be that lump. Then talk back to Bob.

BOB: (Switching, sitting on the pillow.) I am the lump in your throat. I cut you off from other people. You need me. If you get too close to people, if you let them touch you—why, who knows what might happen!

WARD: Switch. Be Bob again. What do you want to say in response to that?

BOB: Need you? Hell, you choke me off, you keep coming back and choking me off! (His body begins to shake.)

WARD: (Moving behind Bob, who is gently sobbing now, putting my arms around his chest, holding him in a viselike grip.) Make a sound.

BOB: (Begins making an angry growl.) Grr. Aahrrr. (More tears.)

WARD: A word. What word goes with the sound?

BOB: Get out of my life, go away, go away! (Sobbing continues.)

WARD: (Still holding the viselike grip.) Now a name. Who are you telling to go away?

BOB: Grr. Ahrrr. (Sobbing begins to subside.) Sandra. Sandra. Ahrr! (Then there is a violent motion, and he breaks my grip on him.) There! Oh that feels good. That feels good. (He sits quietly, looking at the floor.)

WARD: Bob, I'd like to have you put Sandra on the pillow now. Talk to her.

BOB: (Clearing his eyes and beginning to focus on the pillow.) Oh my God, this is difficult (Pause). Go away, don't come back (Said weakly).

WARD: I don't think she heard you. Can you say that louder?

BOB: She heard me all right. Go away. You are no longer part of my life. I'm a priest now (Very weakly).

WARD: I don't think she heard you, Bob (Rather loudly).

BOB: You'll hear me this time! (He suddenly reaches over and grabs the pillow. Lifts it up in the air and slams it to the floor. Then he pounds it furiously with his fists.) Go away, go away, go away, you bitch! Go away! I don't ever want you to come back (very loudly). I won't let you come back!

WARD: Scream it at her.

BOB: (Screaming with almost unbelievable power.) Go away! (More pounding.) We were close once, but you are no longer part of my life! (Then, with a powerful heave, he sends the pillow flying at the wall.) Wow, I do that to myself, (In a weak voice) don't I?

WARD: I couldn't hear what you said.

BOB: (Louder) I said I really do that to myself, to myself, *I* do, *I* bring her back (Faint trace of a smile)!

WARD: Are you aware of what you just did with your face?

BOB: I smiled. That's funny, really. (Then Bob starts to laugh with increasing intensity, until he is rolling on the floor in fits of laughter.)

Bob has come a long way toward awareness of himself and toward spontaneous expressiveness—he almost dares to think that his work is done.

At the next meeting of the group, Bob goes inside himself only to find that the lump is still there in his throat. The chatter between top dog and underdog reaches a fever pitch, after all that work. But somewhere in his center he seems to know what he is still holding back, what he is still avoiding. His avoidance has been so subtle that he had nearly fooled himself.

I say, "Close your eyes and see what scene is there." Bob immediately thought of his father's death, over a year ago. This was a real piece of unfinished business! He had never grieved. He helped other people grieve, but he could not grieve himself. He had been the "cool" priest. He didn't need to cry! It was all in God's hands, in God's plan. *He* didn't need to grieve because God takes care of everything. But now it was as though a voice inside was saying, "But He does not do our grieving for us. That is a human task and *you* are human."

The next several sessions were rough for Bob. He experienced himself avoiding the thing he wanted to do. It was crazy, really crazy, he thought. He would stop the senseless top dog/underdog dialogue only to have it start up again. He felt he was at an impasse. And he was.

WARD: What are you avoiding, Bob?

BOB: Saying good-bye to my father. (He cries and cries.)

WARD: What do you want to say to him?

BOB: (He is working hard to get the words out.) I want to say good-bye. Good-bye (More tears).

WARD: Is there anything else you want to say to him?

BOB: (Crying gently now.) I'm so sorry I wasn't there when you died. I was on church business when I should have been there with you. (Still crying gently.)

WARD: Tell him what you liked about him.

BOB: (Still sobbing gently.) I liked your strength. You were strong.

WARD: Tell him what has happened to you now that he's gone.

BOB: (Still sobbing gently.) It's like my whole world has collapsed now that you are gone.

WARD: Now tell him what you didn't like about him.

BOB: You didn't use all your strength (Still sobbing).

WARD: Be specific.

BOB: (Sobbing harder now.) You drank too much. You should have used more of your strength (Pause). But you didn't know how.

WARD: Is there anything else you want to say to him?

BOB: (Sobbing very softly now.) Just good-bye, you really were a good father and I'll miss you. (Begins drying his eyes.)

WARD: I want you to sit over there opposite the two pillows now and tell me what you see.

BOB: (Moving to a position across from the two pillows.) I see myself over there, beginning to be human. And my tears are over there. I see them as real expressions of my humanness.

WARD: Now what do you want to do?

BOB: (Gently bringing the two pillows together.) I want to bring them together—myself and my humanness. That means my tears are me too.

At the last meeting of the group I say, "Go into your body and see what you are aware of."

Bob is pleased to find that there is no longer a lump in his throat. But he is aware that there is pain in his shoulders. Yet, he feels confident, too. He senses that his work is well underway, and that he will be a better priest for his willingness to work on the pain of being humanness.

Bob's work gives us a glimpse of how the hot seat may be used, and how it was experienced by the pastor. It illustrates the top dog/underdog split as well as showing how hot seat work may progress. In this instance, it ends with some pillow talk. As I have said, there is no cut-and-dried way in which the facilitator is to respond to Bob. He responds in a spontaneous way, helping Bob to claim his experience in the present moment, not just by talking about it, but by experiencing it as fully as possible. Bob is able to change by claiming responsibility for where he is right now. By allowing each Gestalt to move to completion, Bob can spontaneously move to a new place and come more fully into the present as a whole human being. The result that he is in a better position to fulfill his priesthood.

BEYOND THE HOT SEAT

In this chapter I have attempted to look at classic Gestalt work through comments on Gestalt experiments, with brief illustrations of their use. I have focused more extensively on the use of the hot seat. I think that it is important to note, however, that the Gestalt approach utilizes a spectrum of dynamics in relation to groups and individuals beyond the hot seat and beyond the classic experiments.

As Elaine Kepner has pointed out, historically there was a reason for the rather exclusive use of the hot seat at the beginning of the Gestalt approach.[4] It related to the need to train mental health professionals in a new mode of clinical learning. It provided a personal experience for the person in the hot seat. It also provided a demonstration for the other members of the groups—usually beginning counselors and other mental health professionals, including pastors—in how this new approach was actually utilized with a client.

As the Gestalt approach has grown and matured, there has been increasing variation in the nature of Gestalt group experience. A similarity to the group dynamics experience of Kurt Lewin may also be seen. These similarities may be explained by noting that the theories of both Fritz Perls and Kurt Lewin had a common source in the work of the psychologists Kohler, Koffka, Wertheimer and Goldstein. The work of Perls and Lewin moved in quite different directions, however, as Perls focused on the individual and Lewin focused on social systems. Contemporary Gestaltists have realized that neither approach is complete within itself. Therefore they have incorporated group dynamics perspectives into their Gestalt group work, while at the same time maintaining the emphasis on the individual.

Currently, Gestalt groups are putting more emphasis on understanding the group process. Kepner, for example, has identified three stages in ongoing Gestalt groups: (1) identity and dependence, (2) influence and counter dependence, and (3) intimacy and interdependence.[5] Kepner points out, however, that the group is more than a delineation of its dynamics, just as a road map is not the actual territory that it represents. The whole is always more than the sum of the parts.

These types of group experiences allow for interaction of group members according to the general Gestalt rules considered in Chapter 3. They are also often characterized by types of games similar to those we have discussed. Such groups do not develop haphazardly, but may be seen as exhibiting a pattern of movement. Zinker has identified this Gestalt group cycle as consisting of: group sensation, group awareness, group energy, group action and movement, group contact, group resolution, and group withdrawal, rest, and silence.[6] He sees the cycle as continually recurring, with the group moving toward higher levels of awareness and cohesiveness.

If the pastor chooses to do this type of group work, it will be necessary to have both personal experience and training in it. The goal of this type of group experience remains the same as that of the hot seat. It is to help the pastor live more fully in the present and be more fully human, hence, becoming a better pastor.

Being a member of this type of group is the first step toward utilizing it in pastoral work. The second step is getting appropriate training in a recognized Gestalt training program.

Chapter 6

The Royal Road to Integration

DREAM WORK

Ever since Freud stated that "dreams are the royal road to the unconscious," working with dreams has been considered an integral part of psychotherapy. Dreams have also been integral to Christianity. The biblical material is replete with references to dreams. Joseph interpreted the dreams of Pharaoh in Egypt (Genesis, Chapter 41). In the book of Daniel, the word "dream" appears twenty three times (Daniel, Chapters 2, 4, 7). And, of course, it was because of a dream that Joseph took the baby Jesus away and saved his life (Matthew, Chapter 2). Even a cursory examination of biblical material shows that dreams have always been considered very important, and the interpretation of dreams has been an important part of religious life. It is most unfortunate, however, that we do not have details in regard to how dreams were interpreted. It was only a century ago that Freud provided techniques and a modern understanding for dream interpretation.

In his Gestalt approach Fritz also put great emphasis on dreams. Yet his emphasis was different from Freud, as reflected in his statement about dreams: "I believe that it is really the royal road to *integration*."[1] Fritz was originally trained as a Freudian psychoanalyst, and his differences with Freud were not due to a lack of understanding of the Freudian theory. What Fritz objected to was the interpretation of dreams by the therapist. He viewed this activity as having the same basic flaw as the rest of the psychoanalytic technique—it stayed in the middle zone of experience. It was a mental *fitting game,* and little more. Any idea of experience being holistic was missing. Perls viewed the Freudian mental games of interpretation, often based on *free-association,* as contributory to *dis-integration* of the personality. He referred to these activities as fantasy; they were mistaken for reality but were not real because they did not include either the outer zone or the inner zone of experience.

From the Gestalt perspective, working on dreams helps people to become fully alive, complete, and able to enter into life more spontaneously. When our lives are not characterized by spontaneity and completeness, our dreams give us existential messages that can move us toward greater wholeness. But we must be willing to do some hard work in relation to our dreams.

It will help us to understand Gestalt dreamwork if we understand the perspective from which it comes. It begins with the assumption that every part of the dream is the dreamer. Whatever is in my dream is me. It is not the outside reality; it is *my* memory trace, my impression, my projection of the universe. One way of working on dreams is through projection—taking part of oneself and putting it outside and looking at it, experiencing it, and reintegrating it. The goal is greater wholeness, greater integration, increasing self-awareness—something which is a life-long process.

It has been suggested that dreams give us signposts on the endless road to self-awareness. Each image has a rich variety of personal meanings which, if pursued fully, extend to the further reaches of our personal identity and experience. The more we own the discordant and dissociated parts of ourselves, the more our tied-up life is released and our spontaneity increases. The Gestalt approach, including Gestalt dreamwork, seeks to help us finish unfinished situations, fit together the pieces of our personal puzzles, integrate out projections, dislodge our introjections, and turn confluence into contact.

Dreams dramatically reveal where we are on the road to becoming truly authentic, truly alive individuals. Fritz suggested that there are five layers through which we must pass in our life experience.[2]

1. *The cliché layer.* This is represented in simple socializing, such as talking about the weather. No real contact here.
2. *The game-playing layer.* When we are in this layer we play games, fulfill roles (i.e., The good boy. The concerned citizen. The loving pastor). Top dog/underdog games.
3. *The impasse or neurotic layer.* Here we are frozen, stuck. We are becoming aware, but we do not know what to do, how to handle ourselves, or how to respond. Our games aren't working anymore.

4. *The implosive or death layer.* Extending from the previous layer, the defenses are now gone and we are at the center of our neurosis. Our energy, however, is bound up within us. We cannot move.
5. *The explosive or life layer.* When the energy locked up within us begins to move, implosion becomes explosion! Jack Downing suggests that there are five kinds of explosion—grief, anger, orgasm, joy, and ecstasy.[3] There is freedom to experience, feel, and be responsible for.

We are not always in one layer. In our day-to-day experience we often move from layer to layer. Our dreams tell us where we are and, if we can experience their meaning, they help us move forward into increasing integrity and expanding self-awareness.

Fritz said, "I believe that in a dream we have a clear existential message of what's missing in our lives, what we avoid doing and living, and we have plenty of material to re-assimilate and re-own parts of ourselves."[4]

In Gestalt theory dreams come from the ground at the time when figures are not being formed because of the interruption of the thinking processes during sleep. This is another aspect of the function of the middle zone experience, and it allows incomplete gestalten to emerge in the metaphoric language of the dream. From the Gestalt perspective, the existential message of the dream will be missed if it is simply subjected to the rational thought processes. What is needed is interaction with the content of the dream, in a holistic way, so that the metaphoric structures will become clear to us. Our dreams give us a very clear message of what we need to integrate, or reintegrate, into our *now* existence to be more complete human beings.

Perls' approach to dreams was to have the dreamer relive the dream; to bring it to life and let it happen *now,* without interpreting it. If you don't hold back, if you remain open, you will come to experience the meaning spontaneously. Perls' approach was to *be* every part of the dream—every inanimate object, every animate object, and every mood—entering into dialogue with whatever you find in your dream. In doing this you are making contact with projected parts of yourself, parts which have been disowned.

Understanding the powerful force of projection helps us to appreciate the importance of dream integration. Fritz believed that our perception of others or in the world around us is actually a projection. The problem, Perls said, is that our projections are only partial, whereas they should be total. This is how wholeness is attained. In dreamwork the individual seeks to *totally* identify with each and every part of the dream; to totally experience oneself as being everything in the dream.

According to this paradoxical theory, we change by becoming what we are, rather than trying to be what we are not. The same holds true with projections. We reclaim our projections not by taking back what was projected, but rather by identifying totally with the projection. Thus, paradoxically, we are able to reclaim the power that is inherent in the projection, changing alienation into identification.

Dream work allows for the discovery of what Fritz called "holes in the personality." These holes are places where we "go blank." These are the places at which we are *phobic,* so we tend to avoid them. Thus, while Perls advocated doing our own dream work, he also suggested having someone work with us on our dreams. The other person will see the "holes" that we miss and can help facilitate contact with them.

In the remainder of this chapter I will give two examples of dream work I have used in my work as a supervisor of clinical pastoral education. My role in this work was merely that of a facilitator; I helped pastors work on their own dreams and claim the disowned parts of themselves, so that they might achieve greater wholeness—a necessity for effective ministry.

CATCHING THE TRAIN

John was a twenty-six-year-old student from a nearby theological seminary. Following the completion of his second year of study, he entered my program of clinical pastoral education as part of his preparation for ministry in a mainline Protestant denomination. He had earned an engineering degree five years earlier and then served in the United States Navy. It was during his Navy experience that he decided to become a minister. When he left the service he married and enrolled in seminary.

He came to the clinical pastoral education (CPE) experience with high expectations. He wanted to achieve many goals, ranging from learning to be an effective counselor to gaining an understanding of Christian ethics.

He stood out from the rest of the group. He didn't mix well. He volunteered first for almost everything, and in his work with patients he was often overly directive and manipulative. He was also a notably poor listener. He only seemed to feel truly effective when he was "doing something" for a patient.

I had a difficult time supervising John. He disliked criticism of any kind. His usual retort to criticism was, "Well, that's your opinion," smiling as he said this. I found myself disliking John. To me, he was a phony. He had a high-pitched voice and a reddish skin tone which said to me that he was boiling inside, even though he was smiling outside. I felt his compulsiveness was a way of trying to justify himself by "doing." I found myself continually wanting to say to him, "Get yourself together. Pull it together."

I was not surprised when John volunteered to work on a dream. He looked nervous and spoke very rapidly. He seemed to be waiting for my approval to go ahead with his work.

WARD: I don't get the feeling you are saying you really want to work. I experience you as wanting my permission.

JOHN: (Literally jumping from his chair and moving to the center of the group.) I am going to do it!

In this action John has done something very important. He has taken responsibility for himself. But he looks scared. He has never done this type of dream work before.

JOHN: This is a dream I've had over and over again.

WARD: Tell it in the first person, in the here and now.

JOHN: Here and now? (Seems uncertain, scared.)

WARD: Yes, the idea is to recreate the dream.

JOHN: OK. Well, uh, I've had this dream over and over again. But a new twist was in the dream last time. I'll explain. Uh, there's a train coming down the mountain. It's an old steam-type train, ya know (He motions off to the left, ahead of himself). Yeah, well I'm trying to stop the train before it goes to the valley below. I'm kinda halfway between the mountain and the valley, ya know, I try to stop the train, but I never can stop it. It goes right by me, headed for the valley. There's danger there. And then the only way I can do that, stop it, is to climb down the cliff. So I start climbing. And it's cold, and the wind's blowing, ya know. Then there's the new thing, comes in here. I'm climbing down this time with a bicycle on my back. Ya see, I need a bicycle in order to get to the train on time, to stop it, ya know, once I get to the bottom of the cliff, because even when I get there there's still a long way to go. . . . (He trails off, looking at the floor.)

WARD: Well, what happens?

JOHN: Oh nothing. I fall and that's the end of the dream. I always fall. (He smiles.)

WARD: I experience your smile as artificial.

JOHN: Well, that's your opinion.

(At this point several members of the group also corroborate the fact that the smile appears artificial to them, too.)

JOHN: Yeah, well, I wouldn't be smiling if I'd just fell off the cliff, would I? (He seems to say this to himself.)

WARD: What especially interests you about your dream? (John's dream is really fascinating, and I am very intrigued by many aspects of it. But my interest really says more about me than about John. It's better to let him go with what stands out for him.)

JOHN: I don't know, really. The whole thing, I guess. I mean, I've had this dream for so long, so many times.

WARD: (I thought he was going to say that the bicycle was what caught his interest—it was what caught *my* interest.) OK, shall we start at the beginning, then? (John nods his approval. I experience him as eager to get started.) All right, I want you to be the train.

JOHN: Be the train?

WARD: (I experience him as stalling, wanting to be coaxed.) Yes, the train. Start up there on the mountain and come down toward where John is. Be the train.

JOHN: OK. (He moves off toward the left front, turns around, makes two fists, and begins moving his arms and stamping his feet.) Chug! Chug! (Loudly, repeated several times.) Woo, Woo. (Then he makes a charge to where John is and passes right by. All the while, his fists are clenched and his feet are stomping. Then he stops and looks at me.)

WARD: I experience you as wanting my approval to continue.

JOHN: No, I just don't know what to do now.

This is typical for someone doing Gestalt dream work. He still finds it hard to take responsibility for himself, for *his* dream.

WARD: Well, what would you like to do?

JOHN: Go ahead playing the different parts of the dream, like we said (Pause).

WARD: Well? (I refuse to take responsibility for him.)

JOHN: Let's see, where was I? Oh yeah. Well, I'm at the top of the cliff and the train is headed for the valley. I know I've got to stop it. (He looks down as though poised at the top of the cliff.) All right, I'm climbing down the cliff now. (He makes climbing motions.) Then, like I say, this time I have a bicycle on my back. It's stupid, climbing with a bicycle on your back. But I need it in order to get to the train on time once I get to the bottom of the cliff. (More climbing motions.) But it's really cold (Pause).

WARD: Be the coldness.

JOHN: OK, let's see. OK, I'm the cold and the wind. Brr. Whoosh. (While John plays the cold and the wind he seems more alive than before. He really identifies with the cold and the wind.)

WARD: What's happening?

JOHN: That felt pretty real. I got into that, ya know (Pause).

WARD: What's happening now?

JOHN: Well, I fell down—that's the end of the dream.

Having begun to get in touch with some components of the dream, John moves away from his awareness quickly.

WARD: Go back and talk to the coldness and the wind.

JOHN: Talk to—yeah, well I don't know what to say (Pause).

WARD: Well, then just be the wind again.

JOHN: OK, well uh—Brr. Brrrr. (He starts shivering.) I'm cold and strong. I whip against the face of the cliff. (He lashes out.)

WARD: Lash out harder. Harder. Harder!

JOHN: Yeah. (Lashing out.) Take that, and that. Brrr. Whooosh.

WARD: Talk to John as coldness, as wind.

JOHN: I'll fix you. You'll never get to the bottom of the cliff. Brrr. Whooosh. (He makes lashing movements.)

A lot of energy is being projected onto the "coldness." What we are seeing here is a projection of John's own coldness. By playing the coldness, John may come to an awareness of his own coldness, and its strength. This awareness may begin some integration.

WARD: Come over here and be John. (Motioning to where he had fallen down.)

JOHN: (Changing positions.) I don't know what to do with you (talking to the coldness and the wind). I really don't. You always get the better of me. Eventually I lose my grip and fall. (He falls to the floor.) And that's the way it always ends. (He starts to get up.)

WARD: Stay there.

JOHN: What?

WARD: I want you to stay there.

JOHN: OK. (Lays back down.)

WARD: Now close your eyes. You are at the bottom of the cliff. OK? Are you there?

JOHN: Yes, I'm here.

WARD: Are you dead or alive?

JOHN: I'm alive!

WARD: All right, I want you to keep your eyes closed and look around in your valley. Tell us what you see. What are you aware of?

This had actually taken *me* by surprise. I had anticipated more dialogue with the coldness and perhaps an initiation of conversation with the bicycle on John's back. That anticipation says more about where I was than where John was. It also says that perhaps John is closer to moving through his impasse than I had thought. But the purpose here is not to give insight to John or to confirm my own understanding—it is to help John get in touch with his own power, and move beyond the impasse. The fact that he's always falling to the bottom of the cliff and staying there suggests that such a movement is now blocked.

JOHN: It's funny. I'm just experiencing myself as alive. I never thought I'd be alive once I got to the bottom.

WARD: How does it feel to be alive?

JOHN: Yeah, it's wild, but it's really great to be alive. . . .

WARD: Stay with the feeling. What are you aware of now?

JOHN: I'm aware of my body . . . it feels good. And the sun is warm here in the valley. (As he says this he smiles. He has been motionless.)

WARD: Are you aware you smiled?

JOHN: Yes. It was somehow connected with the sun. Like, when the coldness went away the warmth of the sun brought out the smile (Pause).

WARD: What is in your valley?

JOHN: I see green grass everywhere. It's nice here, I like it.

WARD: I thought you had to stop a train.

JOHN: Train? Oh. I'd forgotten about that.

WARD: Can you see the train?

JOHN: No, I don't see it anywhere. (Pause.) (He opens his eyes, starts sitting up.)

WARD: What are you aware of?

JOHN: Nothing, but I feel great.

WARD: OK. I'd like to stop here. Is this all right with you?

JOHN: Yeah.

WARD: Do you feel unfinished with what we just did?

JOHN: No, it's OK.

It is important that John take responsibility for stopping his dream work, just as he took responsibility for starting it.

Recurring dreams are especially important. They push for integration. Frequently, recurring dreams end with great fear being experienced and with a nightmarish quality. They usually speak of great frustration.

We catch a sense of urgency in John's dream. It seems obvious (to everyone except John) that he is alienated from the real sources of power in his life. He cannot stop and get hold of his power, but he makes heroic efforts to do so. He is hindered by his own coldness. He is only now beginning to come to awareness of the strength of his coldness, how it keeps him from his power. Only as he becomes more aware of this can he integrate it and claim his own strength again.

The bicycle that appeared on John's back in the last version of his recurring dream tells us that perhaps John is moving to a point where he will be able to use more of his own power. Had the dream work continued, John would have been asked to be the bicycle, give it a voice, get in touch with it. But only if he really agrees and wants to do it—it has to be meaningful to John.

John appears wide awake as he finishes his dream work. I have a good feeling about it. I sense that he is a little more in touch with himself. Is his struggle toward integration over? Hardly. But dream work is another important step toward John owning his projections and appropriating his own strength, aliveness, and genuineness. He's starting to work through his impasse. He has captured a bit of his strength in a rather surprising way.

He will need all his strength as a parish minister if he is to be maximally effective.

CRYSTAL CHANDELIERS

Joe Jones, a Lutheran minister of thirty-five years, was a searching person. He had done well during his five years as a parish minister. His reason for taking the summer off and becoming involved in CPE was that he felt something was missing inside himself, and he wanted to find out what it was.

Joe was quiet and shy and usually had little to say in any of the CPE seminars. He had always thought of himself as "just a quiet person." As the program moved along, he reported that he sensed things happening within himself, changes which other members of the group verified. For one thing, he was beginning to take risks by working in the hot seat. He was also reaching out in new ways to patients he ministered in the hospital. In a dream seminar, near the end of the CPE unit in which he was enrolled, he volunteered to work on a dream.

JOE: I want to work on a dream.

WARD: OK, go ahead. (The group was, by now, quite familiar with how dream work was done.)

JOE: Well, my wife and I have just bought a new house, and it is a large house. I am really excited as I open the door and go in. It is a bit dimly lit inside, but as I look around I am amazed at the size of the room before me. (Pause.)

WARD: Can you describe the room to us?

JOE: Yes, it is a large room, as I said. High up on the ceiling there are crystal chandeliers. It looks like a palace, but it needs cleaning up. There is quite a bit of dust around, and there are quite a few cob-webs here and there. I'm really getting excited.

WARD: Where in your body are you getting excited?

JOE: I seem to be excited all over, warm all over, like this is the place I always wanted, and I'm coming alive. (Pause.)

WARD: What's happening now?

JOE: I'm upstairs. It seems like there are rooms everywhere. Over here, in one section, there are many rooms with doors closed. Somehow I know what's behind those doors. These rooms seem to be of another time. They are furnished with antique furnishings, oriental rugs. Everything is clean and orderly, though. I get a strange feeling like I've been in these rooms many times before. I don't know how to describe it, just a strange feeling. It makes me feel sort of tingly all over, being near these rooms.

WARD: Are there people there?

JOE: No, there aren't any people there. I sense that people don't belong there. (Pause.)

WARD: What's happening now?

JOE: (After a short silence.) I'm in some other rooms now. They seem to be rooms that someone lives in. I'm in the kitchen. I feel like I've just eaten a full meal. I can even smell the smell of food I like, being in the kitchen. (Pause.) Now I . . .

WARD: What just happened?

JOE: I'm avoiding saying where I am. OK, I'll tell it like it is. I'm in bed with a young woman. I want very much to be there, but I feel a little guilty about it. She wants to have sex with me and I'm holding back. I say to her, "Don't fall in love with me because I can't give you what you want." I feel very bad about this. I'm really scared, I feel myself shaking. I'm shaking. I'm afraid of what will happen if I let myself love her. . . . That suddenly stops. Now I am in a different kitchen, and there is an alarm going off. There is a gas stove over against the wall, and it has an alarm that rings when the fire gets too hot. It's ringing now and I'm trying to turn the stove off. (He moves his hands and arms trying to find a way to turn the stove off.) But I can't find a way to turn the fire off. . . . Now I seem to be in some other rooms. I seem to be blocking right now on what is in these rooms. As near as I can recall, they seemed like rooms I had been in before, in childhood. I am thinking how strange it is that these rooms should be here, in my new house. I recognize several of the rooms. They are rooms that I especially liked in the house I grew up in as a boy.

WARD: How do you feel about these rooms?

JOE: I feel very good about these rooms. I am very happy to find them here (Pause). Now I'm back in the big room. I really am happy about this room. It just seems like a palace, and I begin making plans about what I will do to redecorate, and all the good things that will happen there. (He smiles.) Now I seem to be going away from the house. I see it is quite close to other houses—that surprises me a little. I also notice that you wouldn't . . . *I* wouldn't know the house had all those rooms, just looking at it from the outside. Now I am suddenly noticing that there is a church a short distance from my house. It surprises me a little because it seems to be some kind of Asian church. Then it's like I sort of zoom away into the sky, and the dream ends. (He smiles.)

In that seminar, and in several others before the end of the CPE unit, Joe began to give expression to these inner images and feelings. With considerable animation, he brought to life long-denied aspects of himself.

He reported learning that the fire in his sexual passions was not something that would destroy him. As he came to affirm his sexuality, he began to feel a new connectedness to other people, especially his wife. He showed a fast-growing ability to make connections with his general lifestyle and behavior.

The many rooms in his house thoroughly fascinated him, and he left the CPE unit determined to carry on the exploration of these rooms. During his Gestalt work, he showed less of a tendency to "zoom off into the sky" and a greater capacity to concentrate on his work, moving aside more of the cobwebs and getting in touch with new parts of himself. He began to make connections, both in his dream work and at other times, between the old and the new in his house.

Most central to him was the big room in the house. He came to identify this with his "self," the inner core of his being. He reported that it was a magnificent room, and he began decorating it in creative ways that surprised him as much as it did some of us.

From our pastoral perspective, we see Joe as experiencing spiritual growth. He has begun to get in touch with his inner soul and allow for its growth. This growth is enhanced by his active work in the dream seminar. Here again, we note that dreams are not simply discussed nor analyzed as in some counseling approaches. Dreams are recreated and relived in the present moment. Only then can integration be achieved, helping the person grow in the totality of their being.

Chapter 7

Where the Rubber Hits the Road

At the end of the first chapter, I indicated that I would answer the question of how to help individuals achieve spiritual growth. This final chapter will provide that answer, against the background of the Gestalt approach. I have attempted to show how the Gestalt approach sees the total life experience, the specifics of its theoretical base, and how the pastor experiences the Gestalt approach when she or he works on personal growth. I hope that the reader has gained a clear idea of the figure/ground formation in relation to the Gestalt approach.

The validity of any approach to pastoral care and counseling lies in the results achieved. In the words of Jesus "Ye shall know them by their fruits."(Matt. 7:16, KJV). That is the point at which "the rubber hits the road." Let's talk more about our pastor, Joe Jones.

BACKGROUND

Joe found that as he came to a greater awareness of himself, new relationships began to develop between himself and his parishioners. Individuals increasingly began to seek him out, wanting to talk to him about what was going on in their lives. One such person was a woman we will call Mary. Mary had run into a good bit of difficulty in her life. At one point she had been quite active in the church, but not so during the past year.

Mary came to see Joe for a counseling session two weeks ago. At that time Joe felt a little unsure of himself, and spent most of the session listening. Before his experience in Gestalt he would have been judgmental. He would have spent a lot of time instructing her as to what was right or wrong about her attitudes and feelings, telling her what she ought to believe. This time he had concentrated on becoming fully aware of the person before him. What was happening to her?

What was she feeling? How was she reacting? How was she experiencing her situation, internally?

Joe learned that about three years ago, before he came to the church, Mary was involved in a serious automobile accident that literally changed her life. She had taken a group of young people to a church-sponsored activity and was on the way home when the accident occurred. She suffered a severe back injury that resulted in a prolonged hospitalization. Because she could not return to work soon enough, she lost her job. When she finally was able to return to work again, the only employment she could find paid less money and was the kind of work she hated. Furthermore, she was plagued by continuing pain in her back which precluded her from returning to her original employment, even if the opportunity presented itself. Joe felt she was depressed and angry, but she also seemed to be covering it up with a false façade of bravado. Joe commented on this toward the end of the first counseling session. As the session closed, Mary asked for something to read and Joe gave her a copy of the Reverend Bill Miller's book, *Why Do Christians Break Down?*

After Mary left, Joe asked himself why he had given her this particular book. He decided that he had hoped it would be helpful to her in claiming more of her feelings. He had personally found that book helpful in claiming his own feelings. In the book, Miller points out that we often tend to be afraid of our feelings.

> For instance, if you experience the feeling of anger within yourself and you openly express anger verbally, many people will tell you that you are lacking in self-control and that you should "cool it." If you feel sadness and grief and you openly express that feeling by crying, you are exhibiting a lack of self-control (or worse if you are a male) and someone will tell you you are to "pull yourself together."[1]

Joe realized that this was only too true of many people, and of himself. He had allowed for greater expression of his feelings in his own Gestalt work, and he needed to carry this over into his pastoral care and counseling relationships. For him, this meant two things: He had to correct some of his own theology and change some of his understanding of human behavior.

In terms of his theology, Joe had seen Jesus primarily as a person without any real feelings. He had visualized Jesus as a warm, loving person who always smiled at everything and always said nice things, but as someone who certainly never got angry. What Joe had come to see recently was that Jesus had reacted with real anger when he drove the moneychangers from the temple (John 2:13-16), and that the tears he shed over the city of Jerusalem were real tears (Luke 19:41). These were the things that made Jesus human, and that also make us human. If God really loves us, then God can accept such things as our anger, as well as our love.

From his earlier study of psychology, Joe also had taken in an understanding that open expression of feelings was "acting out," and hence undesirable. What a person ought to do, he had thought, was to sit down and reason things out. He had learned to be analytical. Facts were more important than feelings. Joe knew this hadn't worked for him, and his breakthrough into humanness and authenticity had come only as he had allowed himself to move toward awareness with the whole of his experience. It meant getting into "gut-level stuff." More of the heart, less of the head.

As Mary left at the end of the first counseling session, she stuck her head back in the door of his office and said, "Sometimes I think I am even angry at God for what happened to me." Then she dashed down the hall before he could make any response.

A few days later Mary made an appointment with Joe again. Joe prepared for this session by reviewing what he knew about Mary's situation (there was a time when he would have given little or no thought to a counseling session like this). Reviewing in some detail the previous session, one issue that stood out in his mind was whether he had been "religious" enough. He really hadn't made any theological points or instructed her religiously in any way, and he hadn't ended the session with prayer. What was *religious* about what he had done? And should he have helped Mary to do some Gestalt work on the things she was talking about? He suddenly became aware that he was *rehearsing,* to use one of Perls' terms. Not that there was anything really wrong with that, but it mustn't stand in the way of a truly authentic encounter in the actual session.

THE COUNSELING SESSION

As Mary entered his office Joe thought that she seemed a little more relaxed than she had been before. She seemed eager to get started and she initiated the conversation.

MARY: I read the whole book you loaned me. But I'm not bringing it back yet. I want to reread some parts of it. It was really great. (She seems genuinely enthusiastic.)

JOE: I'm glad you liked it.

MARY: Yeah, well I seem to be feeling a lot better this week and felt a lot more like reading. I usually don't care much for religious books, but that one is certainly different (laughing).

JOE: So, what's different about it? (Joining in her laughter.)

MARY: Well, (hesitating) . . . now please don't take this wrong, but so much of the stuff I've gotten from around the church hasn't seemed to have much to do with real life. I don't mean to be disrespectful or anything, but who cares what some saintly person did hundreds of years ago? I mean, *really*. (Her tone indicates some real anger.)

JOE: Well, I think I might agree with you, at least in part.

MARY: You would? (surprised)

JOE: Yes. Not that it isn't good to strive for high goals, but we are just human beings. Besides, the saints weren't all perfect either.

MARY: They weren't?

JOE: No, they were basically just as human as you or I. They all went through a lot of struggles.

MARY: (Somewhat of a long pause.) Just why did you give me that book anyway?

JOE: I'm not altogether sure. I found a lot in it that was helpful to me. So I can't help wondering what you found in it that spoke to you.

MARY: (Her eyes look cautiously around the room.) It was the whole thing about anger. Dr. Miller says it isn't bad. I was always taught it was really bad to be angry. If I was angry, I was made to go and say my prayers. That used to *really* make me mad. . . . (Her eyes look around the room again, and Joe notices that she has made a fist with her right hand.) It sure made a lot of sense to me, what he said. (Pause.)

JOE: (Responding almost without thinking about what he was doing.) I notice that your eyes darted around the room as you talked about that, and I see you're making a fist with your right hand. Is there something you're angry about right now?

MARY: (Quickly releasing the fist.) You bet there is (Pause). Do you really want to hear about this? (She is becoming increasingly agitated.)

JOE: Yes, if you'd like to share it with me. (Leaning a bit forward in his chair.)

MARY: Well, it has to do with the church. . . .

JOE: That's all right, . . . go ahead.

MARY: (In a louder voice now.) All right, perhaps you've noticed that I almost never go to church anymore. What it has to do with is the place of women in the church. (She pushes rapidly on as though she has to get it out quickly or she will lose her nerve.) I don't mean anything personal about this, you understand, but our previous pastor was really old-fashioned. It's like it was all right for the women to do the tea, or arrange the flowers, but we don't get to preach the sermons or serve in any of the really important positions at all. I'm telling you, I really get madder the more I think about it. (Joe notices she has made a fist again.) The message I get is that the church really doesn't care at all about us women. I go to church and just sit in that pew, and the more I see the men running the show, the madder I get. Who can pray at a time like that? I end up with a backache and sometimes a headache that just lasts for days. I can't understand why the church doesn't care.

Joe notices that there are tears in her eyes and her cheeks are flushed. She is quite agitated, and he finds himself a little scared. He almost expects her to pick up something on the desk and throw it against the wall. She lowers her head a bit, perhaps to hide the tears.

JOE: (Stifling the old tendency to say something like, "Now calm down, why don't we look at how unreasonable you attitude is" or "But let's take a look at all the really good things the church is doing for women.") It's like you are the only one who cares. (He feels he is taking a chance here, that there is quite a bit of confrontation in his statement.)

MARY: (With obvious anger.) You make it sound like *I'm* the one who's responsible, or the only one who has this strange reaction, or something. Oh, I'm not sure what you're saying. I thought you wanted me to tell you what I was really feeling.

JOE: How are you feeling right now? Can you claim it, *right now?* (Said very emphatically.)

MARY: I don't know if I can do that. (Pause.)

JOE: Can you say that you won't let yourself do that?

MARY: Perhaps I could try.

JOE: Try?

MARY: (Her fist is now beating gently on the cushion of the couch on which she is sitting.) Oh, I would like to, I really would. (There are more tears in her eyes.)

JOE: Let your fist say it for you. There, take that pillow beside you, and let your fist do what it wants to do.

MARY: (Almost exploding, and with both fists.) Take that, and that. . . . (With really remarkable strength, Mary pounds the pillow so that dust starts to fill the air.) Oh, sometimes I hate you, hate you (Tears are falling freely now.) How could you do this to me? (Her fists continue to beat on the pillow, and her whole body is involved.) Oh, this feels so good, so good. . . .

JOE: Who are you beating up on?

MARY: (Without hesitating.) Take that . . . why, God, who else? (She suddenly stops.) Oh my God, what have I done? (She now almost literally dissolves in tears, as though she is about to melt into the couch.)

JOE: It's all right. (Said affirmatively, with love, from the heart center.)

MARY: How can you say it's all right (Very angrily)? You're supposed to be a man of God. . . . And you say it's all right? I curse God, and you say it's all right? (More tears.) (A very long pause.)

JOE: (Stifling the urge to defend himself, or God.) Yes, it really is difficult, isn't it? (Pause.)

MARY: (Drying her eyes with a Kleenex, her body seems more relaxed, her hands rest open by her side.) Oh, I'm so sorry, I'm really so sorry. . . .

JOE: Sorry for what?

MARY: I not only got angry at God, but I got angry at you, too . . . and you didn't tell me I was bad or anything like that.

JOE: I feel OK with that, how about you? How are you with that?

MARY: Well, I. . . . (Pause)

JOE: You're not sure?

MARY: Well, I. . . .

JOE: (Forcefully.) Do *you* think you are bad because you were angry at God?

MARY: Well, my father would certainly have been really horrified to see me do what I did. He'd have told me that I would burn in hell for what I did.

JOE: I didn't ask you what your father thought about it, I asked *you* what *you* thought about it.

MARY: Oh, you're right. But my father—

JOE: (Interrupting.) Put your father over there in that chair. (Pointing to the chair beside the couch.) Talk to him.

MARY: What? I don't understand.

JOE: I want you to put your father over there in that chair. Make it as real as you can. Can you picture him over there?

MARY: Yes.

JOE: Describe him to me.

MARY: Well, he's a rather big man. I see him as he was when I was a teenager. He has a large moustache and looks very serious, and he's scowling at me.

JOE: OK, do you have anything that you want to say to him?

MARY: I don't know. . . .

JOE. OK, what is he saying to you? After all, you just beat up on God! Is he pleased or what?

MARY: Oh no, that's why he's scowling. He's very unhappy with me.

JOE: OK, I want you to do something. Go over there, sit in that chair. (Motioning to the chair, Mary rather hesitatingly goes and sits in the chair.) You are your father. Talk to Mary. Your very own daughter has just cursed God. Tell her what you think about that.

MARY: (As her father.) Mary, I just can't believe it. We brought you up to be a good Christian girl. We taught you to say your prayers and to love God. Oh shame, shame, shame. . . .

JOE: Go back over there and respond to that.

MARY: (Back on the couch.) Daddy, how can you say that to me? Sometimes I wonder if you ever were concerned about me at all. You just didn't want *your* ideas upset, you didn't want for *you* to look bad. (She spontaneously moves over to the chair.)

MARY: (As her father.) Don't you talk back to me that way! I'll have respect in this house, I will! (Voice is very strong.) So you not only lack respect for God, but you lack respect for me, your father, as well. You'll burn in hell for that! You'll burn in hell for that! (Very loud and strong voice.)

JOE: OK, back to the other seat. Be Mary.

MARY: (As herself.) Oh, (Very weakly) . . . I don't know what to say to him.

JOE: Tell him that.

MARY: (A little stronger, looking directly at the chair.) Daddy, I don't know what to say to you. I love you very much (Gently sobbing now) and I reach out to you . . . I need you . . . and when I reach out . . . you . . . push me away, and send me to hell . . . I don't know what to say to you (Pause.) (She seems to be processing something inwardly.) Wait a minute, yes, I really do have something to say to you. (She raises up her head, deepens her breathing, and her voice becomes stronger.) You make me really mad! What kind of a father are you?! And I don't believe a word of that religious crap you always dished out to me. That's right! No, I don't believe that God will send me to hell just because I got angry at him! What kind of a God would that be? No, I don't believe that! Well, that may be your kind of God, but it's not mine! (She looks defiant now.)

JOE. Shall we let Daddy respond to that?

MARY: (Pausing.) I don't think he's responding to that. He's drawing back. He doesn't scare me so much now. He even looks smaller (Smiling). (Pause.) Do you want me to go on with this? (Suddenly she looks very tired.)

JOE: No, let's stop here. Does this feel like a stopping point to you?

MARY: Yes, I think so, I really do.

JOE: You've done a lot of work today.

MARY: Yes. . . .

JOE: To really claim your anger against both God and your father the same day is a lot of work. Tell me, how do you feel right now?

MARY: I feel relaxed, I guess. Yes, I really do feel relaxed and, very strange.

JOE: Strange. Can you get more in touch with that?

MARY: You mean the feeling of strangeness?

JOE: Yes.

MARY: Well, I'll try.

JOE: Try?

MARY: (Smiles.) OK. The feeling is . . . tingling. Yes, that's it, tingling. It's going all over my body . . . like I'm coming alive. Yes, that's it—alive, alive!

JOE: Just stay with that feeling (Pause).

MARY: I remember feeling this way a long time ago, when I was a young girl . . . so free . . . alive. I guess I became deader over the years, and then the accident was sort of the final straw. I guess I didn't realize just how angry I was at God. You know, I can't believe it. I just right here, now, sat here and beat up on God. I should feel ashamed. (She smiles a bit as she says this.)

JOE: I thought I noticed a bit of a smile as you said that. (Smiling himself.)

MARY: (Smiling more broadly now.) But this is a whole new idea for me. Hey, here I beat up on God, and you just let me do it. (Smiling even more openly.)

JOE: It's like you just learned something new about God. (Mary nods affirmatively.) And *He* can take it (Smiling).

MARY: Oh honestly, (Begins laughing) I don't think the women's rights thing was really what I was angry about at all. Not that there aren't some real issues there. But I guess I could let anger out there, but not where it really belonged. You know, that's really quite a whole new awareness for me, really (Beaming).

JOE: I rejoice with you in that (Smiling).

MARY: This is still all so new to me. I never did anything like this before (Pause) I'm glad I did it. I always wondered what counseling was all about. Now I think I really know. Who knows, I might even come to church this Sunday. (Smiling, mischievously.)

JOE: Why not come and see if it is still such a pain in the back.

(They both laugh heartily together.)

JOE: But seriously, I do want you to come back to talk with me some more. I think you are beginning to come to grips with some really important things, and there is still more work to be done.

MARY: I'd like to see you next week at this same time. You're right. I've known that I really needed something like this for some time. I guess I just never thought I'd find it in the church.

ANALYSIS

Let's take a critical look at this instance of pastoral counseling done by our pastor, Joe. We will begin with an issue that had been raised by Joe, himself: what was *religious* about the counseling session? At first glance, we might be tempted to conclude that the session was not very religious because the pastor had not said a prayer or "instructed" Mary in any way.

In this regard, it is good to remember a basic distinction between role and function. Role is where our identity is—physician, lawyer, pastor. Function is what we actually do. Studies have shown, in fact, that both pastors and nonpastors, when they are equally trained in counseling, actually perform counseling in almost identical ways. In other words, they "function" in similar ways. Does this mean that there is no difference, then, between pastors and other counselors? No, it does not. The factor that makes the difference is their role. Joe is a *pastor*. This has a profound effect on how he is perceived by others. Since the pastor represents God, there is a qualitative difference in the way he is perceived by others; a difference that is especially significant for church people. A simple word of reassurance, for example, may carry far more weight than the same simple word of reassurance from a nonpastor.

We also need to dispel the old myth that the pastor is only doing something religious when "God talk" is being used. In this regard, pastoral care has indeed "come of age," as pastoral theologians such as Hulme have shown.[2] There is an appropriate place for the use of traditional theological language, but it must take place within the context of the dynamics of the interaction and the relationship between the pastor and counselee. Joe begins where his counsel is, not simply putting her into a predetermined category to which he will respond in a predetermined manner. Today relatively few people communicate through the use of God talk, as was the case in earlier times. The "coinage" of our day seems to be more psychological than religious. The pastor needs to listen to the "language" that the counselee speaks and to communicate in that language. To use God talk with a person who has no familiarity with religion, simply means that there is no communication.

Stated even more basically, we may say that the use of religious words is not the distinguishing characteristic of a pastoral counseling relationship. In fact, we may say that a pastor may use religious words in counseling, and yet there may be little or no pastoral dimension. On the other hand, there may be no traditional religious language used, and yet there may be a very profound pastoral relationship. One of the reasons for this is that communication takes place on more than a verbal level. While dialogue does consist of words, it has many other dimensions beyond words. This is where the Gestalt approach may be helpful in that it emphasizes the nonverbal components of communication. In the counseling session between Joe and Mary, it was Mary's clenched fist that communicated her anger when she had not yet claimed it verbally.

Still another dimension of communication is the pastor's attitude. The pastor may speak of love and acceptance, but does the *attitude,* the nonverbal *behavior,* reflect a judgmental stance? If the pastor cannot reflect love in behavior and attitude, then it should not be surprising if a parishioner does not perceive love. The pastor may verbally give support or reassurance to a person and speak eloquently about the love of God, but if that love is not reflected in the pastor, it may not be grasped at all by the counselee.

A large part of the "coming of age" of pastoral care has been in the recognition of the fact that there is no magic in words, even in theological words. Words are marvelous vehicles with which to symbolize or communicate, but they are not magic. Even the sacraments and other symbols of religion are not magic. They symbolize and celebrate realities in the life experience of people, and apart from that are empty. All theology, in fact, came from human experience and finally must be related back to it.

We presume, and hope, that the time will come for Mary when church attendance will help her celebrate certain experiences in her life. Perhaps she can begin receiving communion again, and find in it her own personal meaning. It may also be that a more traditional "spiritual talk" will be brought into the pastoral counseling relationship with Joe; but all of this must be according to her own need and experience, her own struggle with her life and its meaning.

It is also important to note that what has been said does not preclude Joe from introducing "God talk." However, this must be done within the dynamics of the relationship. We may safely presume that Mary would not have come for counseling from her pastor if she had not expected something "religious," in the very best sense of that word. The use of the traditional religious words and symbols certainly are some of the pastor's most powerful resources.

Let's look more closely at Joe's counseling techniques. How well did he use his Gestalt approach in this encounter? Did he simply bring some "gimmicks" into this counseling session? How did his approach respond to the very personal dynamics with which Mary was struggling?

Certainly, we can begin by complimenting Joe for being able to set aside some of his old counseling habits, such as giving a lot of predetermined advice or answers. He tried to really "see" the person before him; to listen, observe, and to respond to what and who she was. In this sense, he was very much a Gestaltist. He was taking a "I and thou, here and now" stance. We find him open to what might happen—even excited about it.

It is important to note here that there certainly is a place in the church for giving advice and answers. However, they should take their appropriate place outside of the counseling relationship. When the functions of the pastor are inappropriately mixed into the counseling relationship, the counseling relationship suffers as a consequence.

Joe is also observant of nonverbal communication. He hears the tone of voice, he observes the tears and the clenched fist. And, appropriately, he brings these to Mary's attention.

This takes a certain amount of initiative on Joe's part. A strict nondirective stance is not sufficient. Talking about an issue can too easily be an avoidance. Whatever forms of expression the individual exhibits is seen as a movement toward wholeness, toward the completion of a gestalt, and must be attended to by both counselor and counselee. The counselor calls attention, the counselee concentrates on the expression with the goal of awareness. Thus begins the process of discovering the meaning of the experience. Joe's calling attention to the fist, for example, is a beginning of greater expressiveness. Mary immediately unclenches her fist when it is called to her attention. Her initial reaction is to deny, to refuse to claim. Although Mary moved rather quickly to claim this expressiveness, not everyone will move so quickly. If the counselee moves slowly, the counselor must be patient, waiting for the eventual moment when it will be possible for the counselee to claim this expressiveness.

There are, of course, no clearly prescribed ways in which to call attention to expression, and no neat timetable as to when it should be done. As in all of Gestalt work, the Gestaltist has to develop a creative and spontaneous interaction with the counselee.

Once there is an awareness of the manner in which expressiveness is taking place, Gestalt work usually moves to differentiation. At this point, the goal is to help the person claim that part of their experience that has hitherto been disowned. For example, Mary's fist betrayed an underlying anger that she was not claiming. How is it claimed?

She first needs to gain a clearer awareness of what she is doing. She needs Joe to help her in this. The Gestalt counselor assumes that the person coming for counseling has not been able to claim the disowned part by himself or herself—this is why they have come. They are asking for help to do what they have not been able to do alone. Therefore, the Gestaltist uses a basic tool called *experimentation*. These experiments are to help the counselee achieve a clearer awareness of how they are disowning, fragmenting, etc. Experiments may include such activities as exaggerating movements, talking with body parts, or whatever helps the person toward fuller awareness of the "what" and "how" of behavior—which is considered more important than why.

How well did Joe help Mary with the process of differentiating? Perhaps not too well. After initially calling attention to the clenched fist, he moved very quickly to a different type of experimentation that is more characteristic of a later phase of Gestalt work—expressiveness and closure. But we must not be too rash in our criticism of Joe. His technique seemed to work out well, which tells us that he was very much in tune with Mary. We must remember that while there are typical patterns that may be seen in Gestalt work, these are not to be taken as procedural rules.

After calling attention to Mary's fist, Joe might have had Mary simply make the fist consciously. He might have encouraged her to get in touch with how it felt, describe it, make it as tight as possible, to fully experience it in every way possible, and to describe what she was experiencing. He also might have suggested that she talk to that fist, or to give it a voice and let it talk to her. Again, while we must be cautious of our criticism of Joe for not suggesting such an experiment, it is important to point out that if a Gestalt session moves too rapidly, before there has been adequate differentiation, the clarity of the emerging awareness may be diminished.

When an awareness of the "what" and "how" has taken place, the counselee is ready for *affirmation*. That is, the differentiated parts must be claimed. Joe might have suggested to Mary, for example, that she clench her fist hard and say, "I am my fist, I am angry." If at first she does it weakly, he might suggest that she say it again and again, with increasing intensity, until she really "hears" herself saying it. Mary might even have spontaneously added something like, "I am my fist, I am angry, and this is the way I keep from expressing my anger toward God." This may have been a real "aha" experience for Mary, helping her to move toward greater spontaneous expressiveness. With this type of "aha" experience comes a sense of responsibility in relation to this awareness. The organism is now ready to move toward the completion of this gestalt.

The final stage of Gestalt work is *closure*. It is the natural outflowing of the Gestalt work up to this point. In his session with Mary, Joe had rather aggressively suggested an experiment that helped Mary move toward closure. His challenge to her to ". . . let your fist do what it wants to do!" helped her to move toward closure in claiming her anger toward God. This type of experiment can help her stop projecting her anger onto something else—in this case, the cause of women in the church—and see where it is really focused. Only when this happens can she come to any resolution. Otherwise, she will move from one angry battle to another.

This process, however, is usually very complicated. Note, for example, that not only does Mary discover anger toward God, but she also discovers anger toward her father. The roots of her anger run deep. The closure she gains in this session must be seen as part of a larger process, a process that will call for the integration of many fragmented parts.

Closure may take place within a Gestalt counseling session, outside of it, or a combination of both. The closure of each emerging Gestalt is a natural process, and the more a person claims responsibility for the actions of their life involvement, the more the person moves toward a spontaneous life-style that incorporates appropriate gestalt completions.

Each Gestalt counseling session is in a way, a gestalt in itself. Mary, for example, was able to express her anger toward her father in this session, and her feeling of aliveness at the end of the session indicates that she has had some very meaningful closure. However, if her father is still living she will have to decide whether or not to confront him with this anger, and she will need to make choices as to the type of relationship that is appropriate for her to offer him. Closure within the session does not necessarily mean that there is no need for closure outside the session.

How does the Gestalt counselor know if a particular session has been helpful to the counselee or not? In Joe and Mary's case, it would seem that this was a productive session because of the aliveness that Mary reported. The fact that she actually made an appointment to see Joe again is also a good indication of successful work. But Joe will need to be sure that he remains open to where Mary is when she returns for the next session. He may be ready to suggest some new experiments to help her express more of that anger toward her father—only to find that she seems to be at a different place. If he can retain his sense of excitement at *her* process of discovery, keeping the focus on her emerging gestalts, we can be quite optimistic that the counseling relationship will be helpful to her.

From a theological perspective, Joe sees something very important happening in his pastoral counseling relationship with Mary. The tingling of her body and the new sense of aliveness that she reports indicates to Joe that Mary has made contact with the center of her vital awareness. This is her spirit, her soul and it needs to be allowed to grow so that she may claim more of her potential as a creature of God.

It is the affirmation of this inner spirit, and its nurturance toward growth and development, that is the work of the pastor. Joe is seeking to guide Mary into the "spiritual existence" which was referred to in Chapter 1. The goal of all pastoral work is to help persons achieve true vitality and balance in their lives that both they and the larger society may experience life in its fullness, including true spiritual existence. This life is not lived only in the head. It is lived only with the experiencing if our full humanness. Through the full use of all our senses, our actions.

As we have noted earlier in this book, the pastor is interested in more than helping people "get in touch with their feelings." While such an activity is commendable, it must never be an end in itself. There are larger gestalts. In fact, the total life of each person is a gestalt. It begins at birth, progresses through life, and is not complete until death. What will be the overall quality of that gestalt? How much of the God-given capacity of human nature, which is our birthright, will we be able to claim? Each completed gestalt, which we claim in our daily lives, will contribute its part to the larger gestalt of life. This process and the increasing contact we make with the center of our vital awareness leads us one step closer to spiritual growth. The more we are able to transcend our ego, the closer we come to the self, which is the ground of our being.

We also must not assume that the type of Gestalt work Joe did with Mary is going to be the sum total of how he will help her to work for spiritual growth. The church has many time-honored paths to spiritual growth that must not be neglected. The issue is not if they are valid—for surely they are—but rather are they valid for a given person. Is this person ready for them? Do they want them? Joe must be ready for the possibility that when Mary has worked out her anger toward her father, she will stop the counseling relationship and perhaps even drop out of the church. He might also be prepared for Mary to experience her Gestalt work as a spiritual discipline in its own right. She may never need the traditional disciplines to achieve spiritual growth.

Joe, as pastor, stands in a unique relational position in regard to his parishioner. Gestalt has recently put an increasing emphasis on the importance of the relationship between the Gestaltist and the client. Yontef has remarked, "Relational Gestalt therapy has moved to an attitude that includes more support, more emphasis on kindness and compassion in therapy . . ."[3] These are qualities that are inherent in the pastoral role and that will be invaluable in pastoral counseling.

How does Joe, as a person, fit into all this? One thing we know is that he will not be able to contribute to Mary's growth beyond the point of his own personal growth process. Because Joe had been willing to take risks in a Gestalt group, he knew the difficulty in claiming his own humanness. He knew that "living in one's head" was not all there was to life. He knew that the business of being human was tough. There were special difficulties for pastors, but there were special difficulties for other people, too. Basically, however, the claiming of our full humanness is part and parcel of our spiritual task.

When Joe was thinking about his sermon for the coming Sunday, he decided that his title for the sermon would be "We Are Fallible Human Beings." He took as his text words from Genesis 3:5 (KJV), "and ye shall be as gods . . . " The words of the devil! That actually seemed humorous. Taking a text from the devil! The devil promised that we could be gods. We don't have to be simply human beings!

Here is the sermon he preached.

Chapter 8

We Are Fallible Human Beings

Text: Genesis 3:5 ". . . and ye shall be as gods . . ."

What I'd like to explore here are the ways in which all of us, *you* and *I,* try to be gods, ways in which we limit our selves from being fully human, ways in which we make ourselves miserable by not claiming our true natures as fallible human beings. My frame of reference for doing this is my own experience, as well as what I have observed as I have looked around me at other people.

By the way, I hope you will forgive me for the text I took for this sermon. But I just could not resist taking a text that came from the devil! I hope you can see the humor in that. Well, that certainly is a temptation isn't it? There is a seduction in the idea that we might be gods. And perhaps we act more like gods at times than we should. Of course, acting like a god ultimately defeats us as human beings since we cannot really be gods, and to act as though we are is self-defeating to us as human beings.

I would like to suggest that we act more like gods than like women and men (fallible human beings) when we:

1. Deny the reality of our sexuality
2. Think that any other person exists solely for our benefit
3. Think that we always have to have the answers for everything
4. Refuse to admit our responsibility when things go wrong in life
5. Hide our feelings from ourselves and others
6. Refuse to learn from the hard experiences of life
7. Refuse to admit we need other people

1. Denying the reality of our sexuality. Adam and Eve's hiding of their nakedness in the biblical story may be seen as representative of what we have tended to do far too often in the church, and what we do too often in our private lives. We tend to deny, to hide, to ourselves

and others, the most basic fact of our very existence. The attitude, unfortunately, that has often existed in the church is one that has denigrated human sexuality. I think that today, however, we see an increasingly balanced attitude toward sex in the church, in general. Unfortunately, however, here and there we can still find the older denigration of sexuality and judgmental attitudes toward almost any type of sexual expression. Whenever we deny our sexuality, we act more like gods than like human beings.

2. I would like to propose that we also act like gods whenever we think any other person exists solely for our benefit, and when we fail to see and honor the uniqueness of others. The husband becomes a god when he treats his wife more as a servant than as a partner, and the wife becomes a god when she does the same to her husband. Of course, the same thing is true in any relationship. Whenever I think you must meet my every need, respond to my every whim, when I do not recognize or respond to your desires, your feelings, your needs, then I am playing god.

3. Another way of playing god is by thinking that we must always have the answer for everything. Again, the biblical perspective suggests that if we knew all the answers, if we knew all the imponderables of good and evil, we would become gods. We would cease to be human beings. I think that this is one of the hardest things that many of us face. Christians, especially, tend to have a difficult time with this because they often think that the Bible is a textbook that gives all the answers. But I do not think that this is the nature of the biblical material. What we see there is the experience of other human beings like ourselves, their struggles, their tentative answers. This does not mean that God is not revealed in the Bible, but I do not think that God is revealed apart from the lives of real people and, of course, in a special way in the life of Jesus.

I have come to believe, from my own experience, that whenever I feel I have all the answers for myself and others, one or more of several things are happening.

- I have become superficial.
- I don't really understand the true scope of what is happening.
- I come across as judgmental rather than loving.
- I have ceased growing.

Life, in many respects, often remains a mystery to us. We can accept the lack of answers, or not. Being human means that often we do not always know the meaning of good and evil in life. A minister friend of mine wrote a sermon he called, "Living in the Questions." That seems to say it pretty well. Often, the genuine living of life means more questions rather than more answers.

4. One thing that being human means, however, is that we *do* need to take responsibility for those things that happen in life for which we *are* responsible. I don't think that this is ever easy for most of us. We are too eager to take responsibility for the good things that happen, but when things do not go well, we are much more reluctant to take responsibility.

Human relationships being what they are, every relationship in which we are involved brings with it certain responsibilities. Often, when intimate relationships are broken, we tend to project all the blame on the other person. "If only the other person were as ______ (you fill in the blank) as I am, this would never have happened." It really does take a great deal of strength, a great deal of humility, to look at a broken relationship and be willing to recognize the part we played in that brokenness. Whenever we feel that we had no part in it, then we are playing the part of gods. We are perfect!

5. I think we are also acting more like gods than human beings when we hide our feelings. Oftentimes we do just this. We hide our feelings from both others and ourselves. Another friend of mine, right now, is going through a very difficult experience. In the midst of circumstances that would reduce most of us to tears, anger, he always maintains his composure. I suggest that if in all situations in life we maintain our composure, if we never shed a tear, never get angry, then we are gods, not simply human beings. The gods are above such petty things as the expression of feelings!

I think that my friend's difficulty is that he cannot share his feelings because he cannot yet admit them to himself. He seems to be hedged in by a veritable wall of "shoulds" and "oughts." "You should be equal to any occasion." "You should control yourself." "You ought to always be loving and forgiving". "You should never think of yourself," etc. Being at this point means acting more like a god than a human being.

We carry on this god-like stance whenever we are not open to learning from whatever experiences come our way in life, both good and bad. I think that this was one of the most difficult things for me to grasp, personally. I was pretty good at learning from the good things in life. But the bad things that happened to me I tended to look at as tragedies, as injustices that should have happened to no one, certainly not to *me*.

To hold onto such an attitude can lead only to utter despair, depression. But can we not see the godlike quality of this position? *I* should not be touched by this type of human experience. *I* deserve better stuff from life than this! Just like the gods sit on their mountain tops, or clouds, or whatever, unaffected by the afflictions of mortal life, so *I* should be able to sit outside the bad experiences of life and be completely untouched by them! Of course, there is no way I can do this. My only real choice is to learn from my experience or not. And if I choose to learn from it, I may be amazed at what I learn! And one thing that I may learn is that out of my experience of weakness may come some unexpected strength! That is a very old bit of wisdom that is a basic to Christian teaching.

In the clinical pastoral education program I recently participated in, I had this reinforced. I liked the perspective of the program and particularly the group experience which was Gestalt oriented. When we got together we always asked, "What can we learn about ourselves today?" With this attitude, life becomes an exciting adventure, and our growth in the spirit is never ending.

We need other people. I would like to suggest one final thing that we need that the gods do not. We need other people. In a way, this has been implicit in the other things I have been saying that go to make up our nature as fallible human beings. Let me now make it explicit. We need both to care for other people and be cared for by them. I sometimes think it is easier for us to care for others than it is to be cared for by others. Gods do not need to be cared for by others. They are sufficient in themselves. But we are not gods. We are fallible human beings. We do hurt at times. We do need others. We do need the care of others.

Nowhere is this truer than when we experience the breakup of intimate relationships. This is why groups like self-help groups and Gestalt groups are so important. When significant relationships are broken, there are few, if any, of us that can go through the experience alone and find our way to new meaning and new relationships without suffering. Our suffering will be minimized if we are willing to reach out to others. Allowing ourselves to reach out to others is not a sign of weakness. It is a sign of strength.

I think that we, and the church, would be much richer if we claimed more of our humanness. Humanness that includes,

- Having a healthy attitude towards our sexuality
- Recognizing the sacredness of each individual personality
- Being able to live with the unanswered questions of life
- Being responsible for ourselves and our actions
- Accepting and sharing feelings
- Helping people learn from their experiences, bad as well as good
- A mutual exchange of caring

When these qualities are present, I would suggest that we are in a position to become far less like gods than fallible human beings. And we can claim, and rejoice in, our human nature, which we believe God created and, looking at it, declared that it was good!

These are some of the things that I am discovering about what it means to be a fallible human being.

Amen
And so the process of discovery goes on.
Life cannot be tied up in neat little packages.
Continual discovery.
Ever re-newing awareness.
Completed Gestalts being replaced by newly emerging
Ones, moving toward completion.
Discovering new things about ourselves.
—about other people around us,
—about the world around us.
Moving toward a fuller life experience.
Expanding horizons of meaning.
Movement toward full expressiveness.
Tapping more fully the human potential.
Getting in touch with our divinity.
Becoming ready for authentic ministry.

. . . Looking at people, not through a telescope of detached minutiae, but in face-to-face responsiveness to perceive with deeper appreciation the values they are striving in devious ways to attain . . . meeting them at the center rather than the periphery of life's meanings. . . at the center of vital awareness.[1]

Appendix

A Biographical Sketch of Frederick S. Perls, MD, PhD (1894-1970)

The application of Gestalt psychology to the field of personal growth came primarily through Frederick "Fritz" Perls.[1] In understanding this application, it is helpful to know something of his personal life. We will, therefore, look briefly at his life and the development of his theories. As we do this, we will note that his theory and practice grew directly out of his life situation. For him, Gestalt was not only the basis of his work as a psychotherapist, it was his way of life.

Fritz, as everyone called him, was a native of Berlin, Germany. He began studying medicine in Berlin prior to World War I, but the war interrupted it. He entered the German army and served as a medic. He returned to his medical studies following the war to complete the main medical exam in 1920 and received his doctorate in medicine in 1921.

Following completion of his medical studies, he did postgraduate work in Frankfurt, where he was an assistant at the Kurt Goldstein Institute for brain-injured soldiers. It was also at this time, about 1926, that he met his wife-to-be, Laura. During this period, he had contact with existentialists and Gestaltists, although this contact was not a very intensive one. He did, however, have contact with Buber, Tillich, and Scheller. His work with Kurt Goldstein introduced him to Gestalt psychology, but he did not grasp the significance of the Gestalt point of view at that time.

Perls' work with psychoanalysis began in 1925, when he began his intensive training to become a psychoanalyst. At first he worked with Karen Horney, then with Clara Harpel. In 1927, he went to Vienna for supervision work with Helena Deutsch and another well-known psychoanalyst by the name of Hitschman.

He next took up a position in a mental hospital in Germany, but was not too happy in his work. Then, as he says in his rather characteristic way, he wasn't quite sure what he did for a while. There was a period of time when he trained with the psychoanalyst Harnick for about a year and a half. But he felt that Harnick was very sterile so, on the advice of Karen Horney, he went into therapy with Willhelm Reich. It was also at this time that he got his first active patients as a practicing psychoanalyst and that he married Laura and began the process of establishing a home.

As Hitler began his rise to power in Germany, Perls was involved politically in trying to stop him. When the Reichstag burned, Perls said to himself, "You just can't get far enough away from that thing."

At this time Ernest Jones offered him a position of teaching psychoanalyst in South Africa, which he decided to accept. He had previously had an offer from Brill to work in the United States, but he had turned it down. Now he was beginning to see the necessity of leaving Germany. His departure was fortunate; he could not get official permission to leave, but he managed to find a way out that took him and Laura through Holland. He remained in Holland for a time before going to South Africa. During this time he did control analysis with Landau, but it was a time of great hardship and deprivation for Perls and his wife as everything had to be left in Germany. The acceptance of the position in Africa was, however, consistent with his view of the importance of taking risks in life. As he said, "Ernest Jones wanted to know who wanted to go. There were four of us, three wanted guarantees. I said I will take a risk. All the other three were caught by the Nazis. I took a risk and I'm still alive."[2]

His first contact with Freud came in 1936. Although he had previous contact with the Psychoanalytic Institute in Vienna, Perls had not had personal contact with Freud. Perls went to the Psychoanalytical Congress in Marienbad, Czechoslovakia, where he presented a paper, "Oral Resistances," which, he says, was poorly received. When he met Freud during this congress, Freud's tough, rejecting manner particularly disappointed him. In fact, he says he was very much disillusioned.

While in South Africa, he had begun to work on a manuscript, which he titled "Ego, Hunger, and Aggression." He gave this paper to Marie Bonaparte to read and he says she returned it to him saying, "Dr. Perls, if you don't believe in the libido theory anymore, you better hand in your resignation." Perls said that he could not understand what belief had to do with it, as he had not thought psychoanalysis was a religion. Now Perls began to see that the new theories that he was developing were to lead him out of the psychoanalytical camp, and his manuscript was the first statement of a new method. The manuscript was finished in 1940, was first published in South Africa and later, following World War II, was published in London. It has since been published in the United States.[3]

During the time that he was in South Africa, Perls served in the South African Army as a psychiatrist. This was his second period of service in the military. Although he does not say much about these experiences, we may assume that they also helped in shaping his theoretical base. In his work, he also was finding that the traditional psychoanalytic approach had limited effectiveness with many of his patients. He was very much influenced by the holistic thinking of Ian Smuts. When Smuts died, and as the Apartheid movement came to South Africa, Perls felt that it was time to move on, so he came to the United States through Canada. He was not particularly eager to come here because he had been here for a short time in 1923 and did not like it; but he felt that it was the only choice left open to him.

He came first to New York City, but found the heat of the city so appalling that he went on to New Haven, Connecticut. There he found little support from other psychiatrists and was about to go back to South Africa. He was encouraged to stay, however, by Erich Fromm and Clara Thompson, who were associated with the Washington School of Psychiatry. With their encouragement, he went back to New York and within six weeks had a fully booked private practice. While in New York, he, his wife Laura, and others founded the New York Institute of Gestalt Therapy.

Although things were working out well professionally, Perls became increasingly aware of a rather notable theoretical discrepancy between his position and that of the Washington School. He had a good working relationship with the psychoanalysts of the Washington School, but he differed quite radically with Clara Thompson—he could not accept her idea that the adjustment of the person to society was as important as she contended.

It was during this period of time that the book *Gestalt Therapy* was written. Perls had read some of the work of Paul Goodman while he was in South Africa and had been impressed with Goodman's ability to express ideas. So, with Paul Goodman, and Ralph Hefferline, the basic themes of *Ego, Hunger, and Aggression* were given new expression. Experiments were conducted by Ralph Hefferline with his students at Columbia University, and Gestalt therapy was formally introduced to the United States. It is interesting to note that the term "Gestalt Therapy" was coined by Perls somewhat over the objections of some of his colleagues, especially of his wife and Paul Goodman, who had preferred another title such as "Concentration Therapy."

It is fair to say that Perls was somewhat of a wanderer. Although he might well have stayed in New York after the publication of the book, he decided to move on. This move seemed to have been occasioned by several circumstances: (1) the theoretical discrepancies of the Washington School, (2) increasing marital difficulties between him and Laura, and (3) poor health that discouraged him. He went to Miami, Florida, alone. It was at this time that he began to find himself. He had a therapy practice in Miami and also did quite a bit of traveling around the country, mostly giving workshops. Then, as he says, "I was so fed with the whole psychiatric racket, uh, that I went, I just wanted to get away from everything and went on a long trip—14 months, and during this trip I found two places I really liked. One was Kyoto in Japan, one was in Elat in Israel."[4]

Perls settled in Hot Springs, California. At an age when most men have retired, Fritz Perls carried on, deeply immersed in the Esalen movement, active as a psychotherapist, lecturer, and workshop leader. In 1966 Fritz was invited to make a major presentation to the annual convention of the American Psychiatric Association. At last, Gestalt therapy had become legitimate!

In 1969, Perls, now in his late seventies, moved to Lake Cowichan, Canada, where he founded a Gestalt Institute. He next planned for a Gestalt Kibbutz in New Mexico. Late in 1969 he went on his last speaking and workshop tour. He died in a hospital in Chicago in 1970, at the age of seventy-six.

Since the early founding of the Gestalt Institute of New York and the founding of Esalen, numerous institutes have been founded in the United States where the Gestalt approach is practiced and taught. In the latter part of the twentieth century, Gestalt was said to be the fourth most popular approach to counseling/personal growth in this country. As the twenty-first century begins, we see a resurgence of interest in the Gestalt approach around the world, and an increasing number of Gestalt Institutes being formed.[5]

Perls said, "I have been called the founder of Gestalt therapy. That's crap." Still, history will, without a doubt, continue to confer that honor upon him.[6]

Notes

Chapter 1

1. Paul E. Johnson, *Psychology of Pastoral Care* (New York: Abingdon, Cokesbury, 1953), p. 8.

2. Charles F. Kemp, *Physicians of the Soul* (New York: The Macmillan Co., 1947).

3. Orlo Strunk, "Psychotherapy" in Rodney J. Hunter (Ed.), *Dictionary of Pastoral Care and Counseling* (Nashville: Abingdon Press, 1990), pp. 1022-1027.

4. Frederick S. Perls, *Ego, Hunger, and Aggression* (San Francisco: Orbit Graphic Arts, 1966).

5. Frederick Perls, Ralph Hefferline, Paul Goodman, *Gestalt Therapy: Excitement and Growth in the Human Personality* (New York: Dell, 1951).

6. For an excellent compilation of resources in relation to Gestalt see: Chris Hatcher and Philip Himelstein (Eds.), *The Handbook of Gestalt Therapy* (New York: Jason Aronson, Inc., 1976), pp. 779-796. For other resources consult the Web page: <http://www.gestalt.org>.

7. Claudio Naranjo, "Gestalt Therapy as Transpersonal Approach," *The Gestalt Journal* (Fall, 1978), pp. 76-77.

8. M. Miller and J. Miller (Eds.), *Harper's Bible Dictionary* (New York: Harper and Brothers, 1952), p. 197.

9. James Lynwood Walker, *Body and Soul* (New York: Abingdon Press, 1971).

10. Dietrich Bonhoeffer, *Creation and Fall,* trans. by John C. Fletcher, (New York: Macmillan Co., 1959), p. 47.

11. For an interesting presentation that gives a Gestalt perspective on sacraments see: Miles Renear, "Gestalt Therapy and the Sacramental Experience," *The Journal of Pastoral Care* XXX:1 (March, 1976), pp. 3-15.

12. John B. Cobb Jr., *Theology and Pastoral Care* (Philadelphia: Fortress, 1977), p. 12.

13. Naranjo, "Gestalt Therapy," pp. 75-81.

14. Usharbudh Arya, *Superconscious Meditation* (Prospect Heights, IL: Himalayan International Institute of Yoga Science and Philosophy, 1974).

15. William Johnson (Ed.), *The Cloud of Unknowing* (New York: Image Books, 1973), p. 103.

16. Cobb, *Theology,* pp. 5-9.

Chapter 2

1. Chris Hatcher and Philip Himelstein (Eds.), *The Handbook of Gestalt Therapy* (New York: Jason Aronson, 1976).

2. Erving Polster, Miriam Polster, *Gestalt Therapy Integrated* (New York: Brunner/Mazel, 1973).

3. Frederick Perls, Ralph Hefferline, and Paul Goodman, *Gestalt Therapy: Excitement and Growth in the Human Personality* (New York: Dell, 1951).

4. Vernon Van de Riet, Margaret P. Korb, John Jeffrey Gorell, *Gestalt Therapy: An Introduction* (New York: Pergamon Press, 1980).

5. Frances Tustin, *Autistic States in Children* (London, Boston: Routledge and Kegan Paul, 1981).

6. Victoria Hamilton, *Narcissus and Oedipus* (London: Routledge and Kegan Paul, 1982).

7. Polster and Polster, *Gestalt Therapy Integrated.*

8. Frank Goble, *The Third Force* (New York: Grossman Pub., 1970).

Chapter 3

1. Frederick S. Perls, *Gestalt Therapy Verbatim* (Lafayette, CA: Real People Press, 1969), p. 1.

2. Abraham Levitsky and Frederick S. Perls, "The Rules and Games of Gestalt Therapy," in Joen Fagan and Irma Lee Shepherd, *Gestalt Therapy Now* (Palo Alto, CA: Science and Behavior Books, 1960), pp. 70-76.

3. Aubrey Yates, *Behavior Therapy* (New York: John Wiley and Sons, Inc., 1970), p. 64.

4. Arnold Beisser, "The Paradoxical Theory of Change," in Joen Fagan and Irma Lee Shepherd (Eds.), *What Is Gestalt Therapy?* (Palo Alto, CA: Science and Behavior Books, 1970), pp. 110-116.

5. Leland Johnson, *Pillow Talk* (Houston: The Gestalt Institute of Houston, n.d.).

6. Frederick Perls, Ralph Hefferline, and Paul Goodman, *Gestalt Therapy: Excitement and Growth in the Human Personality* (New York: Dell, 1951).

7. Phillip Kapleau, *The Three Pillars of Zen* (Boston: Beacon Press, 1965), pp. 64-65.

Index

Page numbers followed by the letter "f" indicate figures; those followed by the letter "t" indicate tables.

Aboutism, 14
"Acting out," 87
Actual, feeling the, 58-60
Adam and Eve
  projection, 16, 52
  and sexuality, 103-104
Adam-adamah (man-earth), 7
Affirmation, pastoral counseling, 98, 99
Alienation, Gestalt perspective, 47
American Psychiatric Association, 112
Anger
  claiming, 86, 90, 93, 98-99
  Gestalt perspective, 73
  pastoral counseling session, 87, 88, 90, 91-93, 98-99
Answers, playing God, 103, 104-105
Anxiety, Gestalt experiments, 41
Apple, directed awareness experiment, 60-61
Assimilation
  directed awareness experiment, 60
  Gestalt perspective, 4
Attachment, confluency spectrum, 23t, 24
Attention
  Gestalt equation, 4
  Gestalt technique, 38
  pastoral counseling, 97
Attitude, pastoral counseling, 95
Authenticity
  in folktale, 53-54, 56
  Gestalt experiments, 41-42
  Pastor Joe Jones, 87
Awareness
  Gestalt experiments, 41-42
  Gestalt perspective, 4, 13, 24, 57-58
Awareness *(continued)*
  Gestalt technique, 38, 39
  pastoral counseling, 97
Awareness continuum, Gestalt perspective, 33, 34
Awareness techniques, Gestalt experiments, 41

Behavior therapy, counseling techniques, 29, 30
Being, Christian perspective, 7
Body
  Christian perspective, 7-8
  Gestalt perspective, 33, 34
Bonaparte, Marie, 110-111
Bonding, confluency spectrum, 22, 23, 23t
Bonhoeffer, Dietrich, 8
Buddhism, 10
Burber, Martin, 3, 32, 109

Caring and humanness, 107
Carter, Chester, pastoral care, 10-12
Catching the train, dreamwork, 74-80
Change, views of, 30
Chemotherapy, 1-2
Christian perspective, 6-8
  on dreams, 71
  and Gestalt perspective, 8-10
  and time, 25-26
  and transpersonal experience, 48
Cliché layer, life experience, 72
Client-centered therapy, 1, 2

Clinical pastoral education (CPE) program, self-criticism, 45-46
Closure
 Gestalt perspective, 4, 13, 21
 pastoral counseling, 97, 98, 99
Cloud of Unknowing, The, 10
Cobb, John B., Jr., 9, 10, 11-12
"Coming of age," pastoral care, 94-96
Communication
 Gestalt perspective, 32, 33
 nonverbal, 95
"Computers," mind as, 5, 9, 45, 64
Concentration
 Gestalt perspective, 25
 pastoral counseling, 97
"Concentration Therapy," 112
Confluence, 16, 19-24, 23t
 in folktale, 51-52, 55
 Gestalt experiments, 41
Contact
 in folktale, 55
 Gestalt perspective, 4, 13, 57, 58
Contact and withdrawal, Gestalt technique, 38
Contact-boundary, Gestalt perspective, 47
Countertransference, 27
Crystal chandelier, dreamwork, 80-83

Daniel, dream of, 71
David, hunger of, 5
Defense mechanisms, 18
Deutsch, Helena, 109
Diagnosis, Gestalt perspective, 14-15
Dialogue game
 in folktale, 55
 Gestalt technique, 35
Differentiation
 Gestalt perspective, 4, 19
 pastoral counseling, 97
 spectrum of, 22-24, 23t
 and spiritual life, 20
Directed awareness experiment, 60-62
Dispassion, 10
Displacement, defense mechanism, 18
Dream integration
 in folktale, 55
 Gestalt technique, 40, 71-72
Dream interpretation, psychoanalytic technique, 30, 71
Dreams, Christian perspective, 71
Dreamwork, Gestalt, 72, 73-74

Earth, human nature, 7
Ecstasy, Gestalt perspective, 73
Ego
 Gestalt perspective, 46-47
 psychodynamic approach, 43
 and self, 48
 and spiritual growth, 9, 10
Ego, Hunger, and Aggression, 3, 110, 112
Ellis, Albert, 43, 44
Encounter groups, 1, 2
Energy, Gestalt perspective, 18-19
Environmental contact, Gestalt experiments, 41
Esalen movement, 112
Exaggeration, Gestalt technique, 38-39
Excitement, Gestalt perspective, 57, 58
Experience
 blocking of, 15-24
 Gestalt perspective, 13-15
Experimentation, pastoral counseling, 97
Explosion
 five kinds of, 73
 in folktale, 55
Explosive/life layer, life experience, 73
Expressiveness
 in folktale, 56
 Gestalt perspective, 4, 13
 pastoral counseling, 97, 98
Exterior zone
 CPE, 46
 Gestalt perspective, 43, 44f

Fantasy
 DMZ, 43
 Gestalt perspective, 71-72
Fantasy journeys, Gestalt technique, 39-40
Father, anger at, 91-92, 93, 98-99
Feeling the actual, Gestalt experiment, 58-60

Feelings
 claiming of, 86, 90
 and humanness, 107
 playing God, 103, 105
Figure, Gestalt perspective, 4, 43, 47
Fist
 nonverbal communication, 95
 pastoral counseling session, 88-89, 98
Fitting game, 71
Folktales, in Gestalt therapy, 51-56
Fragmentation, 7-8
Frankfurt Neurological Institute, 3
Free association, psychoanalytic technique, 30, 71
Freedom, Gestalt perspective, 13, 26
Freud, Sigmund
 defense mechanisms, 18
 on dreams, 71
 and Perls, 110
 psychodynamic elements, 43
 on the therapeutic relationship, 27
Fromm, Erich, 111
Function, 94
Future, Christian perspective, 26

Game-player layer, life experience, 72
Games, Gestalt perspective, 29, 35-39
Gestalt counseling session, 99
Gestalt equation, 4
Gestalt experiments, 41-42, 58
Gestalt group work, 69
Gestalt Institute, 112
Gestalt perspective, description of, 4-6, 30
Gestalt techniques, 30-41
Gestalt therapy, 3
 neurosis, 57
 popularity of, 112-113
 projection, 16-17
Gestalt Therapy, 3, 111-112
Girard, Robert, 9
Goble, Frank, 26
God
 anger at, 87, 90, 91, 93, 98-99
 attachment confluency, 24
 interactional confluency, 24
"God talk," 95-96
Goldstein, Kurt, 3, 109
Goodman, Paul A., 3, 111-112
Gossiping, Gestalt perspective, 32-33
Grandiosity, identity lines, 24
Grief, Gestalt perspective, 73
Ground
 and dreamwork, 73
 Gestalt perspective, 4, 43, 47
Group action and movement, Gestalt group cycle, 69
Group awareness, Gestalt group cycle, 69
Group contact, Gestalt group cycle, 69
Group energy, Gestalt group cycle, 69
Group process, Gestalt perspective, 69
Group resolution, Gestalt group cycle, 69
Group sensation, Gestalt group cycle, 69
Group withdrawal, rest, and silence, Gestalt group cycle, 69
Growth, Gestalt perspective, 4, 56
Growth stagnation, Gestalt perspective, 57-58
Guilt, 37

Harpel, Clara, 109
"Head trip," 9
Heart, Christian perspective, 6
Heaven, Christian perspective, 7
Hefferline, Ralph, 3, 112
"Holes in the personality," 74
Holistic approach, use of, 2, 7, 9
Horney, Karen, 109, 110
Hot seat
 Gestalt technique, 40
 pastors training, 62-68
Hulme, William E., 94-95
Human nature
 Christian perspective, 6-8
 Gestalt perspective, 13-14, 46
Humanness
 claiming of, 107
 denial of, 103-104
Hunger, Gestalt perspective, 4

I and Thou
Gestalt perspective, 32, 33
pastoral counseling, 96
I have a secret, Gestalt technique, 37
I take responsibility
in folktale, 54
Gestalt technique, 36
Id, psychodynamics, 43
"Ideal behaving," 23
Identity
and confluence, 22-24, 23t
and dependence, Gestalt group process, 69
Impasse/neurotic layer, life experience, 72
Implosion, in folktale, 53
Implosive/death layer, life experience, 73
Individuality
claiming of, 20
in folktale, 55
Infant, confluence bond, 19
Infatuation, and confluence, 22-23
Influence and counterdependence, Gestalt group process, 69
Integral Psychology, 9
Integration, Gestalt experiments, 41-42
Intellectual activity, and Gestalt perspective, 14
Interactional confluence, confluency spectrum, 23t, 24
Interactional end, confluency spectrum, 22, 23t
Interior zone, Gestalt perspective, 43, 44f
Intimacy and interdependence, Gestalt group process, 69
Introjection
blocking mechanism, 16, 17-18
and confluence, 21
directed awareness experiment, 60
in folktale, 52, 55
Gestalt experiments, 42

Jesus
claiming individuality, 20
human feelings of, 87
Last Supper, 8-9
life of, 14
Jesus *(continued)*
Lord's Prayer, 25
ministry of, 18
on results, 85
on the soul, 6
John, dreamwork, 74-80
Johnson, Paul E., 1, 2, 41
Jones, Ernest, 110
Jones, Joe
dreamwork, 80-83
pastoral counseling, 87-94
pastoral counseling analysis, 94-101
pastoral counseling background, 85-87
Joseph, dream of, 71
Joy, Gestalt perspective, 73

Kemp, Charles, 1
Kepner, Elaine, 68, 69
Kurt Goldstein Institute, 109

Labeling, in Gestalt perspective, 15
Last Supper, 8-9
Learning
and humanness, 107
playing God, 103, 106
Lewin, Kurt, 68, 69
Life
five layers of experience, 72-73
Gestalt perspective, 3, 48
"Living in the Question," 105
Lord's Prayer, 25

Magic Wall, The, 49-51
Make the rounds, Gestalt technique, 35
Marriage, and confluency, 20-21
Mary
background, 85-87
counseling session, 87-94
May I feed you a sentence?, Gestalt technique, 39
Mental illness, Gestalt perspective, 5
Middle zone (DMZ)
CPE, 46

Middle zone (DMZ) *(continued)*
  and dreamwork, 73
  Gestalt perspective, 43, 44f, 45
Miller, Bill, 86
Mirroring, confluency spectrum, 23, 23t

Naranjo, Claudio, 6
Nephesh, 7
New York Institute of Gestalt Therapy, 111, 112
Nonverbal behavior
  pastoral counseling, 95
  pastoral counseling session, 95, 96
Now, principle of, 32, 43, 96

Onion, peeling of, 29, 42
"Oral Resistances," 110
Organism, in Gestalt perspective, 6, 33, 46
Orgasm, Gestalt perspective, 73
"Orienting the self," Gestalt experiments, 41

Paradoxical theory of change, 30
Past, Christian perspective, 25-26
Past-life experience, 25
Pastor, anger at, 91
Pastoral care
  Chester Carter, 10-12
  "coming of age," 94-96
Pastoral counseling
  and communication, 95
  and psychoanalytic method, 26
  and Rogerian counseling, 26
Pastoral education
  catching the train, 74-80
  crystal chandelier, 80-83
  directed awareness experiment, 60-62
  feeling the actual experiment, 58-60
  hot seat experiment, 62-68
Pastors
  role of, 94-95, 100
  work of, 1, 10, 100
Paul, 6
Perls, Fritz (Frederick S.)
  on blocking mechanisms, 16
  on closure, 21
  on dreams, 40, 71-72, 73
  on ego function, 47
  experiential focus of, 44
  "holes in the personality," 74
  hot seat experiment, 62
  on human nature, 6-7
  life of, 3-4, 5, 109-113
  on life's five layers, 72-73
  on neurosis, 57
  on peeling the onion, 29
  on projection, 16-17, 73-74
  and psychoanalytic community, 109-111
  on responsibility, 21
  on his role, 113
  on the self, 47
  on theory, 49
  on the unconscious, 15-16
  vocabulary of, 4, 5, 6
Phobias, Gestalt perspective, 74
Phobic behavior, in folktale, 53
"Physician of the soul," 1, 56
Pillow talk
  Bob, 65-66, 67, 68
  Gestalt technique, 41, 55
  pastoral counseling session, 90
  Paul, 63
Playing the projection, Gestalt technique, 37
Polster, Ervin, 14, 21
Polster, Miriam, 14, 21
"Power in the present," 24
Precognition, 25
Present, in Gestalt perspective, 24-27
Primal therapy, 1, 2
Projected identification, 21
Projection
  blocking mechanism, 16-17
  and confluence, 21
  and dreams, 73-74
  in folktale, 52, 55
  Gestalt experiments, 42

Projection *(continued)*
  Gestalt technique, 37
Pseudoquestions, Gestalt perspective, 34
Psycho synthesis, 9
Psychoanalytic Institute, 110
Psychoanalytic model, 1, 13, 43
  counseling techniques, 30
  defense mechanisms, 18
  and dreams, 71
  and pastoral counseling, 26
  success of, 26-27
Psychodynamic elements
  Gestalt perspective, 43-48, 44f
  psychoanalytic model, 43
Psychological health, Gestalt perspective, 47
Psychology, models of, 1-2
Psychosomatic illness, Gestalt perspective, 18-19
Punishment, behaviorist technique, 30

Rational-emotive therapy, 1, 43-44
Reaction formation, defense mechanism, 18
Rehearsal
  Gestalt technique, 38
  pastoral counseling session, 87
Reich, Willhelm, 110
Relational Gestalt therapy, 100
Relationship
  Gestalt perspective, 32
  playing God in, 103, 104, 106-107
Religion
  and experience, 13
  and Gestalt perspective, 8
Repression
  defense mechanism, 18, 46
  Gestalt perspective, 58
Resentment, identity lines, 24
Responsibility
  dreamwork, 75, 77, 79
  in folktale, 55
  Gestalt perspective, 13, 21
  Gestalt technique, 36
  and humanness, 107
Responsibility *(continued)*
  pastoral counseling, 98
  pastoral training, 64
  playing God, 103, 105
Retroflection
  blocking mechanism, 16, 18-19
  and confluence, 21
  in folktale, 52, 55
  Gestalt experiments, 42
Revenge
  and confluence, 22
  identity lines, 24
Reversal, defense mechanism, 18
Reversals, Gestalt technique, 37-38
Reward, behaviorist technique, 30
Rogerian counseling, and pastoral counseling, 26
Role, and identity, 94
Roles, in folktale, 52
Rules, Gestalt perspective, 29, 31-35
Rules and games, 29, 42

Sacredness, recognition of, 107
Secrets, Gestalt technique, 37
Self
  and confluence, 19, 21-22
  definition of, 9
  and ego, 48
  Gestalt experiments, 41-42
  Gestalt perspective, 46, 47
Self-regulation
  in folktale, 51
  Gestalt perspective, 48
Self-transcendence, 10
Senses
  exterior zone, 43
  Gestalt perspective, 4, 57, 58
Sexual behavior, and confluence, 22
Sexuality
  denial of, 103-104
  and humanness, 107
Soul, Christian perspective, 6-7
Spirit
  Christian perspective, 6
  pastoral care, 10-12
"Spiritual existence," 99-100
Spiritual growth, 9, 10, 48, 62, 83, 85, 100

"Spiritual talk," 96
Spirituality
  Christian perspective, 9, 61-62
  and confluence, 19-20
  in Gestalt perspective, 5, 61
Stagnation, Gestalt perspective, 58
Strunk, Orlo, 1
Superconscious, 9
Superego, psychodynamic model, 43

Techniques, therapeutic, 29, 30
Therapy
  confluency spectrum, 23-24
  forms of, 1-2
"There is a time for everything under the sun," 13
Thinking, DMZ, 43
"Third Force, The," 26
Tillich, Paul, 3, 109
Time, concept of, 25
"Top dog vs. underdog," 62, 64
Transaction, Gestalt perspective, 4
Transference, psychoanalytic technique, 27, 30
Transpersonal experience, and Christian perspective, 48
Transpersonal Gestalt, 9
Trust, confluency spectrum, 23-24

Unconscious, 15-16
Undoing, defense mechanism, 18
Unfinished business
  in folktale, 53
  Gestalt perspective, 5, 46
  Gestalt technique, 36-37
  pastoral training, 66

Vital awareness, 1, 2, 7
  in folktale, 53, 56
  pastoral counseling, 99, 100, 108

Washington School of Psychiatry, 111
"We Are Fallible Human Beings," sermon, 101, 103-108
Why Do Christians Break Down?, 86
Withdrawal, Gestalt technique, 38
Women's rights, pastoral counseling session, 89, 93

Yates, Aubrey, 29
Yontef, Gary, 100

Zinker, Joseph, 69

Order a copy of this book with this form or online at:
http://www.haworthpressinc.com/store/product.asp?sku=4549

PASTORAL COUNSELING
A Gestalt Approach

_______in hardbound at $39.95 (ISBN: 0-7890-1531-5)
_______in softbound at $24.95 (ISBN: 0-7890-1532-3)

COST OF BOOKS______

OUTSIDE USA/CANADA/ MEXICO: ADD 20%____

POSTAGE & HANDLING________
(US: $4.00 for first book & $1.50 for each additional book) Outside US: $5.00 for first book & $2.00 for each additional book)

SUBTOTAL________

in Canada: add 7% GST____

STATE TAX____
(NY, OH & MIN residents, please add appropriate local sales tax)

FINAL TOTAL____
(If paying in Canadian funds, convert using the current exchange rate, UNESCO coupons welcome.)

☐ **BILL ME LATER:** ($5 service charge will be added)
(Bill-me option is good on US/Canada/Mexico orders only; not good to jobbers, wholesalers, or subscription agencies.)

☐ Check here if billing address is different from shipping address and attach purchase order and billing address information.

Signature________________________________

☐ **PAYMENT ENCLOSED:** $________________

☐ **PLEASE CHARGE TO MY CREDIT CARD.**

☐ Visa ☐ MasterCard ☐ AmEx ☐ Discover ☐ Diner's Club ☐ Eurocard ☐ JCB

Account # ______________________________

Exp. Date_______________________________

Signature_______________________________

Prices in US dollars and subject to change without notice.

NAME____

INSTITUTION_____________________________________

ADDRESS____

CITY____

STATE/ZIP_______________________________________

COUNTRY_______________________ COUNTY (NY residents only)_______________________

TEL___________________________ FAX___________________________

E-MAIL__________________________

May we use your e-mail address for confirmations and other types of information? ☐ Yes ☐ No
We appreciate receiving your e-mail address and fax number. Haworth would like to e-mail or fax special discount offers to you, as a preferred customer. **We will never share, rent, or exchange your e-mail address or fax number.** We regard such actions as an invasion of your privacy.

Order From Your Local Bookstore or Directly From

The Haworth Press, Inc.

10 Alice Street, Binghamton, New York 13904-1580 • USA
TELEPHONE: 1-800-HAWORTH (1-800-429-6784) / Outside US/Canada: (607) 722-5857
FAX: 1-800-895-0582 / Outside US/Canada: (607) 722-6362
E-mail: getinfo@haworthpressinc.com

PLEASE PHOTOCOPY THIS FORM FOR YOUR PERSONAL USE.

www.HaworthPress.com

BOF00